THE JEWISH QUARTERLY

The Jewish Quarterly is published four times a year
by The Jewish Quarterly Pty Ltd
Publisher: Morry Schwartz

ISBN 9781922517166 E-ISBN 9781743822784
ISSN 0449010X E-ISSN 23262516

ALL RIGHTS RESERVED.

No part of this publication may be reproduced, stored in a retrieval system
or transmitted in any form by any means electronic, mechanical, photocopying,
recording or otherwise without the prior consent of the publishers.

Essays and reviews © retained by the authors

Subscriptions 1 year print & digital (4 issues): £42 GBP | $56 USD.
1 year digital only: £25 GBP | $32 USD. Payment may be made
by Mastercard or Visa. Payment includes postage and handling.

Subscribe online at jewishquarterly.com or email subscribe@jewishquarterly.com
Correspondence should be addressed to: The Editor, The Jewish Quarterly,
22–24 Northumberland Street, Collingwood VIC 3066 Australia
Phone +61 3 9486 0288 Email enquiries@jewishquarterly.com

The Jewish Quarterly is published under licence from the
Jewish Literary Trust Limited, which exercises a governance function.
UK Company Number: 01189861. UK Charity Commission Number: 268589.
Directors of the Jewish Literary Trust: Lance Blackstone (chair),
John Cohen, Andrew Renton and Michael Strelitz.

Founding Editor: Jacob Sonntag.

Editor: Jonathan Pearlman. Associate Editor: Jo Rosenberg. Literary
Editor: Natasha Lehrer. Sales and Marketing Coordinator: Therese Hava.
Management: Elisabeth Young. Design: John Warwicker and Tristan Main.
Production: Marilyn de Castro. Typesetting: Typography Studio.

Cover image: President of Ukraine / Flickr; image on p.73: *Exterior view of
Jewish National Library, Kadimah and Celia Crosby Memorial Hall*, c. 1941,
photographer: Lyle Fowler, State Library of Victoria

Note on previous issue: In "The Jews of Singapore", a quote from Chief Rabbi
Mordechai Abergel did not convey the intended meaning. The quote in digital
versions has been updated to: "The local Iraqi Jews of Singapore have intermarried
into the wider Jewish community and made other connections."

Issue 251, February 2023
THE JEWISH QUARTERLY

Contributors   v

Vladislav Davidzon The Jews of Ukraine:
Baal Shem Tov to Zelensky   1

David Herman *The Jewish Quarterly* at seventy   50

History
Harvey Belovski The Rambam and his brother   64

Community
Tali Lavi The dybbuk in the room:
Melbourne's Yiddish art scene   70

Reviews
Jakub Nowakowski Is Poland really forgetting
its amnesia?   83

Devorah Baum The myth of the Jewish literary mafia   98

Contributors

Devorah Baum is a writer and filmmaker, and teaches English Literature at the University of Southampton. Her new book, *On Marriage*, will be published this year.

Harvey Belovski is the senior rabbi of Golders Green Synagogue in London, rabbinic head of University Jewish Chaplaincy and a writer and BBC broadcaster.

Vladislav Davidzon is the founder and former editor of *The Odessa Review*, a non-resident fellow at the Atlantic Council's Eurasia Center, a contributor to *Tablet Magazine* and *Foreign Policy*, and the author of a new book on Jewish–Ukrainian relations.

David Herman first wrote for *The Jewish Quarterly* in 1981. He lives in London, and is a regular contributor to many publications, including *The Times Literary Supplement* and *The New Statesman*.

Tali Lavi is a critic, writer and public interviewer, and a programmer for Melbourne Jewish Book Week.

Jakub Nowakowski is the director of the Galicia Jewish Museum in Kraków, Poland.

The Jews of Ukraine
Baal Shem Tov to Zelensky

Vladislav Davidzon

No contemporary reckoning with the millennium-long history of Ukrainian Jewry can commence without acknowledging the obvious: the nation is now fighting for its very survival. This war is being waged by a committed, fearsome and obsessive adversary – a country that cannot let go of its traumatised past, with a leader who has desperately staked both the legitimacy of his regime and his political future on the bloody reconstruction of a bygone empire. Yet if the Soviet empire is now experiencing its final gasps and dying twitches, the Russian war against Kyiv has revealed certain erroneous suppositions widely held by many of us – specifically, those of us post-Soviet citizens who had assumed we had avoided Yugoslav-style bloodshed through a peaceful dissolution of the Union. (This includes me: I was born in Uzbekistan during the first days of Perestroika to Russified Ukrainian Jews who had been evacuated in 1941 ahead of Hitler's advancing armies.) The war to escape Russian domination, it turns out, had merely been put off for several decades. In September 2022, the Jewish-Ukrainian businessman Victor Pinchuk opened his annual star-studded Yalta European Strategy political conference in Kyiv by explaining to the assembled dignitaries that the Ukrainians had been operating on the false assumption that they had won independence:

> We thought that we had gotten independence in 1991, but it turns out that we had only gotten it formally; it is a very expensive thing independence, and it works only if it is paid for in full. The breakdown of the empire has not really happened yet, and a dinosaur can take a very long time to die.

The blitzkrieg coup de main that Russia commenced on 24 February 2022 was waged under the ideological pretext of the "denazification" of Kyiv. In other words, the stated justification for the invasion – which the Kremlin continues to call a "military operation" – was to wipe out the allegedly revanchist fascist junta ruling Kyiv. Ukraine is a pluralist liberal democracy; the attempt to decapitate the government and replace it with friendly proxies was based on all sorts of miscalculations by autocratic Russian president Vladimir Putin, but perhaps the worst part is that he seems to have believed his own propaganda about the Ukrainians.

Thus it is both a remarkable historical irony and a quotidian fact of contemporary Ukrainian life that its dashing wartime commander-in-chief is a Ukrainian gentleman of Jewish descent. Volodymyr Zelensky – a former comedian, producer and actor who hails from the Russian-speaking south-east of the country – has never hidden or downplayed his Jewish heritage. Indeed, Ukraine's history of ethnic strife and antisemitism did not prevent 73 per cent of the Ukrainian population from voting for the political novice in the 2019 presidential elections, making him only the second Jewish head of state in the world at that time. Zelensky and the Israeli president have since been joined in the rarefied club of Jewish world leaders by another post-Soviet head of state: Egils Levits, president of Latvia, an arch supporter of Ukraine who appeared at Pinchuk's conference with bombs dropping around him. This perhaps intimates that the post-Soviet phenomenon of multi-ethnic national belonging is a regional trend (as is the corollary desire for cleansing the national sense of shame through revisionist World War II history). The election of Zelensky was fascinating exactly for how ordinary it all seemed to Ukrainians at the time, and for how little his being a Jew had mattered during the presidential campaign. He had even casually made ribald jokes about it. ("I will send my Jewish mother after you!" he threatened his opponent, incumbent president Petro Poroshenko during one of their debates.) The banner of contemporary Ukrainian civic nationalism – one based not on ethnic or linguistic definitions of regional belonging but rather on values and mentality and national pride – was being carried by a slight, muscular Jewish comedian from a Russian-speaking part of the country.

> *As in much former Soviet territory, many Ukrainians might find at least some Jewish lineage if they cared to look for it*

This sort of political and social equanimity has not – to put it mildly – been the historical norm. As it happens, Jewish heritage was until very recently considered to be a serious liability in Ukrainian presidential elections. The case of former Ukrainian prime minister Arseniy Yatsenyuk is instructive. Slim, exceedingly tall, prematurely bald and bespectacled in the manner of a hipster Western technocrat, Yatsenyuk was one of the most talented Ukrainian politicians of his generation. Possessing a deep sense of self and a sinewy sort of swagger, he was the shooting-star wunderkind of Ukrainian politics and had already served as economics minister, foreign minister and speaker of the parliament before his thirty-fifth birthday. In 2010, at the age of thirty-eight, he threw his hat into the ring for the presidential election.

The systematic repression of all religions by the officially atheist Soviet state, in the service of moulding the citizenry into a singular and universal ideal, had made intermarriage common. As in much former Soviet territory, many Ukrainians might find at least some Jewish lineage if they cared to look for it. Also, like in other Holocaust-shaped and post-communist European countries in Central Europe, there has been a wide array of responses to dealing with Jewish heritage among the Ukrainian political class. Many Ukrainian politicians of Jewish descent are discreet about it; others embrace their Jewishness publicly and proudly. Still others deny it altogether.

The idea that Yatsenyuk – who resembled a suave French *fonctionnaire* rather than a grim Soviet-style apparatchik – was of covert Jewish descent was injected into the Ukrainian political discourse in an ingenious and amusing fashion. A political operative working for one of his opponents commissioned a pair of Jewish scholars to produce a mostly serious book on the "Fifty most renowned Jews of Ukraine". It was a slim volume with a blue cover decorated with a Magen David and portraits of Jewish Ukrainian luminaries, including the Kyiv-born Golda Meir and the Odessa-born Isaac Babel. The most prominent photograph was naturally the one of the young Yatsenyuk. Tucked inside the volume was a rather florid entry describing the imagined grandeur of Yatsenyuk's alleged Jewish heritage – he was said to be a direct descendant of "the family that had penned the Talmud". Five thousand copies of the volume were duly printed, sparking a whisper campaign that soon constituted a political liability. Yatsenyuk was attacked by one of his most vicious and nasty populist opponents as being an "impudent little Jew" and a "thief".

Yatsenyuk finally decided to squelch the murmurs. He turned to a senior Ukrainian rabbi – the American-born Yaakov Dov Bleich (full disclosure: Dov Bleich is a family friend) – and asked him to publicly dispel the rumour. Bleich complied, informing both the local and international press that even though Yatsenyuk "was a very nice guy and very much a worthy candidate for the Ukrainian presidency", he was "certainly and most definitely not a Jew". Whether the episode was the reason for Yatsenyuk not advancing into the second-round run-off in the presidential elections is a question best left to the historians – but some of his opponents, at least, certainly assumed that being Jewish would be an electoral liability. Yatsenyuk, in any case, was voted in as the prime minister four years later in the wake of the Revolution of Dignity.

> *The accomplishments and identities of Ukrainian Jews almost always belonged to other national histories*

In 2017, I found myself in the ballroom of one of Ukraine's finest hotels – sitting across the table from Yatsenyuk amid a lunchbreak during his Kyiv Security Conference. My own grandmother was born in a shtetl outside Yatsenyuk's hometown of Czernowitz (part of Romania between the two wars) and, like most every other civilised person whose ancestors hail from that region, I harbour a nostalgia for the aesthetics and rule of the Austro-Hungarian Empire. After a boozy lunch and some lively banter over our mutual affection for the Austro-Hungarians, I worked up the courage to ask Yatsenyuk for the truth. Was he or was he not a member of the tribe? Yatsenyuk waved the question away in his usual cavalier fashion: "I never thought to ask my mother about it!"

Jews in Ukraine and Ukrainian Jews

The uncertainty about Yatsenyuk's lineage is symptomatic of the elusiveness of any attempt to delineate the tremendously rich and ancient history of Ukraine's Jews. Ukrainian Jews are in many ways a new phenomenon because the Ukrainian state in its current form is a modern creation. The accomplishments and identities of Ukrainian Jews almost always belonged to other national histories. In that way, Ukrainian Jewish history resembles the broader Ukrainian national history and is a microcosm of it – each has simultaneously existed and not existed over the course of many centuries. Occupied, effaced, partitioned and continually expunged out of existence as a separate nation, Ukrainians have been ruled successively by Turks, Poles, Lithuanians, Germans and Russians. And all the while, they engaged in continuous – and often doomed – national rebellions. Jews have also lived with them, in the lands of the Slavs, for centuries during their suppression – the often-systematic repression of the Ukrainian nation, its culture and language – and have been targeted by parallel suppression.

It should be acknowledged that all different kinds of Jews have lived in these lands. Many now viewed as "Ukrainian Jewish" certainly would not have thought of themselves as such at the time. For most of the last millennium and a half, a Jew who spoke a language other than Yiddish or Hebrew would be as likely to be conversant in a Turkic dialect as in any Slavic tongue. Later there would be Jewish contributors to Ukrainian-language literature, even as Ukrainian became viewed in Russian imperial and chauvinist circles as the language of peasants and country bumpkins (a view that has sadly lingered in modern times). Hrytsko Kernerenko, for instance, was perhaps the first serious Jewish poet to have published good verse in Ukrainian in the 1890s.

The Ukrainian search for a usable past in the context of statelessness is an instinct that should be instantly familiar to contemporary Jews, who likewise only received national statehood in the twentieth century. That search can be seen in recent Ukrainian attempts to reclaim various artists, writers, poets and filmmakers who have long been assimilated into the canons of the Soviet or Russian avant garde. Though the current war has suspended Ukrainian civil aviation, a movement to rename Kyiv's Borispol international airport after Kazimir Malevich has been gaining support in recent years. (Malevich, who painted the archetypical black square into "Russian art history", was actually an ethnic Pole from Kyiv.) In certain pleasing cases – such as the pioneering Soviet filmmaker Dziga Vertov and his cinematographer brothers, Boris and Mikhail Kaufman – a personality can be reclaimed for both the Ukrainian and Ukrainian Jewish canons. Why, Ukrainians understandably ask, should these figures be taught in university art courses under the rubric of Russian modernism?

Since the Russian war against Ukraine began, Jews all over the world have found themselves re-examining their identities. Being a "Russian Jew" has become an uncomfortable and unattractive marker as Russia becomes even more of an internationally toxic pariah state. Similarly, many American, Canadian, French or British Jews who had always thought of themselves as Russian have revisited their family histories and noticed that the towns in which their ancestors lived were in fact in Ukraine. The majority of Ashkenazi Jewry can trace their ancestry back to Ukraine as well as to Russia – where their ancestors usually wound up only after the nineteenth century.

In fact, any attempt to delineate a particularly "Ukrainian" Ukrainian Jewish history – especially one that existed prior to the sixteenth century – often involves making capricious or contestable judgements about which Jewish histories, movements, artworks, facts or personages to assimilate into that history. A prominent rabbi, politician or poet might have been born on the wrong side of the Hungarian imperial border, or in the Belarusian lands annexed to the Polish–Lithuanian Commonwealth, and so might be retroactively ascribed to German, Russian, Polish or Ukrainian history or culture. My own paternal grandmother was born into a Romanian shtetl and became a Soviet citizen before being evacuated through Moldova to Central Asia by the Soviets, finally dying an American citizen in Brooklyn. I have often thought of a particular poet, artist, rabbi or actor as an example of "Ukrainian Jewry" only to learn from their Wikipedia entry that they were born somewhere in Russia, Moldova or Belarus before making their contribution to whatever vocation or craft in Ukraine. The category of the "Ukrainian Jew" is thus elusive, mutable and all too modern.

Ancient roots in Crimea

The history of Jewish life in Ukraine – that is, of the Jews who have lived in the lands bounded by the current Ukrainian borders – is most easily thought of as consisting of three discrete civilisations. There are contemporary Ukrainian Jews – who are the product of the same Ashkenazi Eastern European culture as the Jews of Poland, Belarus, Moldova and Germany. Going further back, there are the Turkic-origin Jewish populations who lived in the south of Ukraine and the Crimean Peninsula (that is, in lands that never fell under the dominance of Kyivan Rus'). These are the Krymchaks and the Karaites – of whom the Krymchak population survived and flourished as a separate group, until the Holocaust. And then there is the most vanishingly ephemeral: the quasi-mythical Middle Ages kingdom of the Khazars.

Any discussion of the Jews living in the territory of the former Russian Empire or in the contemporary Ukrainian lands must begin with the remarkable and much disputed history of the Khazars. The kingdom of those semi-nomadic Turkic traders buffeted both the Byzantine Empire and the Muslim realm. At least a portion of the ruling Khazar elite – according to Jewish and Arab historical sources – converted to some form of Rabbinic Judaism in either the eighth or ninth century. Whether the story is true, or which of the Khazar elites actually took up Judaism, remains

"Whoever tells you that he or she has found 'the Khazar gene' is a charlatan"

almost entirely lost to history, as does the question of whether the rituals that they practised constituted Jewish practice by any modern standard. Their political structures remained essentially medieval Turkic, with a military king sharing power with a figurehead "sacred" king who would eventually be ritually strangled to death. "When we say 'Khazars adopted Judaism', we cannot be certain who we are talking about – Khazars proper, or also their ethnic relatives of Alans, Volgan Tatars and Eastern Slavs," writes Israeli historian Dan Shapira. "We simply don't know and never will. Whoever tells you that he or she [has] found 'the Khazar gene' is a charlatan." We also have little understanding of which language was spoken by the Khazars; their now lost imperial tongue was perhaps a variant of Turkic before many of them assimilated and began to use proto-Slavic.

Medieval Spanish philosopher Judah Halevi's claim that the political elite of the Khazars had converted to Judaism by 740 is now widely disputed. What we do know is that the Khazars superseded the polity of their near ethnic kinsmen – the Bulgars – and went on to forge one of the vastest states in the Europe of their day. Khazaria's borders spread over swathes of contemporary Ukraine all the way to the Caucuses, assimilating all sorts of tribes into their multi-ethnic polity. It became a hub of regional trade, specialising in providing protection to and taxing the merchant caravans that would pass through it. The Khazars later promulgated a pair of lengthy and very nasty wars with the Arabs in the seventh and eighth centuries – wars some historical sources suggest may have prevented the further spread of the Arab world into Europe.

Some Judaised sections of the Khazars are thought to have relocated to Eastern Europe in the wake of the collapse of the Khazarian state. They are now a sort of mythical people – for some, the archetype of ancient "real Russian and Ukrainian Jews", and for others, the source of antisemitic conspiracies "proving" that Ashkenazi Jews do not possess historical or genetic links to the land of Israel. Various contemporary genetic studies seem to corroborate centuries of Eastern European folk wisdom: though the Khazars are not in fact the direct progenitors of the bulk of modern Eastern European Jewry, some of their bloodlines seem to have been assimilated into the wider family of Ashkenazi Jewry.

Beyond the Khazars, the ancient history of Ukrainian Jewry can be traced back to the intrepid seafaring merchants who first set foot on the coast of the Black Sea – known in ancient times, almost two millennium ago, as the Pontic. Those Jews were assimilated into the Greek colonies that had sprung up along the coasts of the peninsula. Now known as the Krymchaks (literally "inhabitants of Crimea" in Russian), these communities eventually used Turkic tongues. For centuries they continued to practise forms of Rabbinic or Talmudic Judaism that might be familiar to contemporary Jews. The Krymchaks formed the core of the population we now consider the indigenous Jewry of the Crimean Peninsula. They grew grapes and made wine, and engaged in regional trade. They also reportedly practised polygamy – until fairly late, by the standards of European Jewry. Mostly rejecting intermarriage, the Krymchaks and their descendants lived in those lands for a millennium and a half, until the 1940s, when their communities were decimated at the hands of the Nazis.

In the ninth century, the stolidly anti-Rabbinic Karaites – often described as "sectarian" in origin – arrived in the Crimean port town of Theodosia after passing through the Holy Land from Persia. The purist Karaites rejected modern Jewish law and would countenance no modern interpretations of the Torah outside of the core texts and practices proffered by Moses. Instead, they focused on spiritual interpretations of the texts. The Karaites forged communities side by side with the Krymchaks, but relations between these diaspora brethren were often acrimonious: sharing a peninsula with distant cousins is never easy. Ironically, both groups engaged in more even-keeled relations with the Muslim rulers of the Crimean Kaganate. Turkic rulers of the peninsula – whether the Khazars or, later, the local ruling faction of the Golden Horde – protected and tolerated the Jews while levying taxes on them. At the same time, the Jewish population of the peninsula was soon reinforced by communities of Jews who fled coerced conversion amid renewed religious fervour among the Byzantine emperors.

By 1475, the subjugation of the majority of the Crimea Peninsula by the Ottomans essentially turned the peninsula – and its Jewish inhabitants – into feudal subjects under the sultans. Over the course of several centuries, the Karaites became ever more assimilated into Turkish culture. They began a radical evolutionary shift away from Jewish rites and cultural practices in the middle of the nineteenth century. The full embrace of their Turkish roots ironically spared them elimination during the Shoah: after a great deal of confusion and historical study, the Nazis pronounced the Karaites to be not ethnically Jewish – unlike the Krymchaks, whom they proceeded to murder.

Before that happened, however, swathes of the Karaite diaspora spread into the northern parts of the Lithuanian–Polish Commonwealth, where, in parallel to Ashkenazi communities, they were granted the economic concessions and social privileges known as the Magdeburg rights. As in Crimea, the Lithuanian branch of the Karaites alternatively competed economically and engaged socially with the local Jewish communities. The centuries of the Polish–Lithuanian Commonwealth would be remembered in many ways as a prolonged golden era for Eastern European Jewry. Jews streamed into the polity from all over Europe whenever they came under threat in other European lands. I still occasionally meet Ukrainians with dark hair and eyes who believe their ancestors were Karaites or Krymchaks from the Crimean Peninsula.

Askenazis and Cossacks

The Jewish history in the Ukrainian steppes – the lands that today make up the northern and central parts of Ukraine – was markedly different. This was an Ashkenazi history, and the communities there are assumed to have arrived from the German-speaking Czech lands of Bohemia and Moravia. Slavic historical sources speak of Jews engaging in business and residing in Kyiv as early as the tenth century, but we have much less knowledge of them. Their community inaugurated the Jewish tradition of residing in Kyiv's Podil district – which, much like the Marais in Paris, would retain its outsider, Jewish, hipster and often sexual outlier identity into modern times.

The Kievan Letter, discovered in the Cairo Genizah, is the best known and most useful account of that era in our possession. It was a formal petition by community leaders on behalf of a Kyivan resident who was looking for ways to pay off his debts (he seemed to have been robbed; his life savings had been purloined). The earlier Kyivan Rus' Jewish communities had been Slavic speakers, yet the later influx of Jewish émigrés from the German "mittleEuropean" lands of Central Europe essentially Yiddishised the bulk of those communities (that is, outside the Turkish-speaking communities of Crimea). By the sixteenth century, a swathe of the Kyivan Rus' lands – including in the region of Galicia – had been merged into the Polish–Lithuanian Commonwealth. The Jews of Eastern Europe now found themselves divided over several national polities, governed by the Khans and the Polish-Lithuanians. The political status, cultures, language preferences, freedoms, identities and rights of European Jewish communities varied significantly.

> *The "Baal Shem Tov" created a new form of worship that would transform Eastern European Jewry*

The events that transpired next are crucial for understanding the next 300 years of Jewish, Ukrainian, Russian and Polish life and relations. In 1648, the Ukrainian hetman (or commander) Bohdan

Khmelnytsky led an uprising of the Zaporozhian Cossacks and their Turkic Tatar allies against the combined military forces of the Polish and Commonwealth Confederation. It was a war the Cossacks would win. They would also engage in rampaging bouts of methodical violence against the Ukrainian communities of Eastern Europe. The Khmelnytsky Uprising marked the return of – or, depending on one's politics, the foundation of – modern Ukrainian self-rule. The Cossacks forged an identity of freedom-loving, tough, autonomous Ukrainians that underpins Ukrainian political life to this day, along with a streak of anti-authoritarianism and anarchy that sets them apart from the Russians.

The Khmelnytsky Uprising was accompanied by horrific pogroms – organised bouts of vicious violence against both the Catholic clergy and Jewish communities. At that moment, around a third to half of all the Polish Jews were living in the territory of the modern-day Ukrainian lands. They found themselves without political allies. The slaughter of entire communities of Jewish civilians would take place unless they could get to a friendly Polish fortified garrison or city in time to seek protection (and in certain cases to take up arms – the myth that Russian and Ukrainian Jews never fought should be dismantled wholesale). When the peasants and their Cossack allies breached the walls of a town, they would not take as prisoner any members of the Polish nobility, Jews or Polish Catholic clergy – all were murdered.

By 1654, Khmelnytsky was ready to accept peace with the Russians to his eastern flank, signing the Treaty of Pereiaslav. This turned out to be a fatal miscalculation, as the Cossacks lost more and more autonomy to the tsars over time. The nasty relations with the Poles engendered by the wars lingered on until the 1990s, and Khmelnytsky still inspires ambivalence among many

Ukrainian patriots for having given the state over to the Russians. The decimation of those Jewish communities was perhaps the worst pre-Holocaust attack on Jewish communities in European history and caused the Jews tremendous trauma. While the scholarly arguments about the number of Jews killed in the massacres are contested – accounts of that time are now widely thought to have exaggerated the number of Jewish victims – it was certainly in the tens of thousands. Even centuries later, the Khmelnytsky Uprising remains one of the predominant stains on the history of the Jewish–Ukrainian relationship.

Birthplace of Hasidism

The Cossack rampages coincided with and in many ways led to a tremendously fecund period of Jewish revival across the Ukrainian lands. Israel Ben Eliezer, the "Baal Shem Tov", born around 1700, was the seminal figure of the mystical revival. He was an itinerant holy man – one of many rabbis of this sort who would travel around offering blessings and hawking holy trinkets as well as legal and spiritual services. But Ben Eliezer created a new form of worship that would transform Eastern European Jewry.

Hasidism – or "piety" – emerged as an energetic backlash to the dogmatic, schematic and didactic forms of worship into which traditional Jewish Orthodoxy, especially in Lithuania, had congealed. This was a doctrinal evolution that prioritised joyful and ecstatic worship – praying while dancing vigorously and living ascetically replaced what some viewed as excessive and rigorous study in the yeshivot. This was a mystical folk religiosity, a shift to the piety of the simple Jewish worker that created a serious split in the world of Eastern European Jewry. It also led to two centuries of religious change. Those opposed to Hasidism, the Misnagdim, were so afraid of this dangerous new movement and the potentially schismatic split in Judaism that they in effect called on the secular authorities to intervene.

The Baal Shem Tov chose Dov Ber ben Avraham of Mezeritch as his successor to lead the movement. He codified many of his guru's teaching into popular writing, helping the movement spread from western Ukraine to the Hungarian countryside. Within a hundred years most Jews in what is now western Ukraine were Hasidim. It was a major reset of Eastern European Jewish practice.

Although this riposte to the Eastern European rabbinic establishment was a kind of anarchic hippie gesture, half a century later (around the start of the nineteenth century) the Hasidim essentially reverted to prioritising the study of the canonical texts and commentaries, even adding an entire textual literature of their own. Every insurgent mysticism must eventually be tamed by tradition and institutionalised, and this was no different, as the movement splintered into individual sects, each with their own particular teachings and led by a class of charismatic hereditary scholar-leaders. This is why, when you see a Hasidic man in Brooklyn, you can identify from which town in Ukraine or Hungary his particular Hasidic sect originates by the cut of his silk caftan or the shape of his fur hat.

Odessa and the Russian Empire

While Hasidism was revitalising and reordering Jewish life across Eastern Europe in the eighteenth century, the Russian Empire was in the midst of the swiftest imperial expansion in human history. The tsars finally succeeded in subjugating and ultimately partitioning the Polish realm. While annexing huge swathes of these territories, the tsars accumulated hundreds of thousands of Jewish subjects they had little idea what to do with. They decided to sequester the Jews in zones outside the main Russian cities. In 1791, the Pale of Settlement was established in the periphery of the Russian Empire. The vast majority of the tsar's Jewish subjects lived there and were not allowed residency in the towns and cities further to the east – with the remarkable and important exception of the port of Odessa.

Founded by Catherine the Great as a free-trading port on the Black Sea, Odessa constituted a unique experiment in autonomy, multiculturalism and cosmopolitanism within the autocratic Russian empire and consequently has had an outsized influence on Ukrainian, Russian and Jewish history.

Odessa's status as a nineteenth-century cultural hub was legendary

Odessa (I have always considered the Ukrainian spelling – *Odesa* – to be wrong for linguistic, historical and etymological reasons, even if I have to defend this position against Ukrainian patriots who understandably see it as pro-Moscow) never allowed serfdom but did allow anyone – including Jews – to settle there. It thus quickly evolved into being the freest place in the empire; its status as a nineteenth-century cultural hub was legendary, even by the standards of other cosmopolitan port cities.

Odessa was erected by Europeans and remains the most glamorous city in Ukraine. Its cobblestone Italianate streets and Venetian Gothic Revival architecture were designed by Italians and Greeks, and its first several governors were French. It has always attracted a class of hustling international adventurers to its ruling elite. Russian was its lingua franca, but for most of its history ethnic Russians were a minority within its fluctuating demographics. It is still peopled with numerous nationalities – the most cosmopolitan city in the most ethnically diverse region of Ukraine, and a Black Sea gateway to Constantinople.

The city was a safe cradle for the creation of new movements and ideologies. With the exception of Theodore Herzl, almost every major early Zionist had either lived here or passed through the town – certainly Ze'ev Jabotinsky, but also Ahad Ha'am and Meir Dizengoff, who became the first mayor of Tel Aviv. The roster of cultural figures the city has produced is legion. This included the entire Odessa school of classical music. Odessa's iconic gangsters and anarchic figures were immortalised by the twentieth-century writer Isaac Babel. He wrote in Russian, but contemporary Jewish literature also took root in the city with the work of Mendele Moykher Sforim and his disciple Sholom Aleichem. Listing the accomplishments of Odessan writers, artists and musicians is the work of a lifetime – I edited a monthly magazine devoted to that pastime for several years, and had the sense of only having gotten started. The city is just remarkably fertile – one of my writers speculated that it was due to a magical concoction of salt in the air, but the reasons remain inscrutable.

Over the course of the nineteenth century, the Jewish subjects of the tsar gradually and methodically transformed into Russian Jews. They were first drafted into the Russian army in 1827 – and to this day, Belarussian, Russian and Ukrainian Jews all recall the fact that Jewish communities were required to give up allotments of boys to the army. These boys had to convert to Russian Orthodoxy and spend the next twenty-five years serving the tsar in the Russian army, only then being allowed to retire and live in the towns. Many of these Russian Jewish men would lose touch with their Judaism.

By the 1860s, even as most of the empire's Jewish population continued to live fairly hardscrabble lives, a small but fairly visible portion of the Russian imperial Jewry was steadily becoming more educated and increasingly entering the white-collar professions. The economic success of these Jews began to generate resentment among other parts of the population, which – again – should not detract from the fact that most of the Jews in the Russian Empire were destitute and lived in shtetls outside the city. A few lucky Jewish merchants who possessed the wherewithal and connections at court to receive concessions became fabulously wealthy and integrated into the Russian ruling classes. Some even acquired titles of nobility or had their Austrian or French titles acknowledged by the Russian imperial courts. Philanthropists such as Israel Brodsky – who bequeathed his name to the Kyiv Synagogue – as well as grand families such as the De Gunzbourgs would become elegant fixtures at the highest levels of society in St Petersburg.

By the second half of the nineteenth century, the Russian Empire was in its regnant phase, as well as its decline. It was also home to various utopian and revolutionary movements – the old order, quite manifestly, could not hold. Tsar Alexander II was assassinated in 1881, which augured the beginning of terrible times and mass reprisals against the Jews of the empire. The renewed urban tensions culminated in a wave of pogroms across Ukraine. These pogroms were repeated at the end of the nineteenth century, leading to a wave of mass migration of Jews from the Russian Empire to America, British Mandate Palestine and, to a lesser extent, Western Europe.

By far the most important of these pogroms was the Kishinev massacre of 1903 – two days of the most frenetic violence that one can imagine that would supercharge the nascent ideology of Zionism and predicate further Jewish immigration to the New

World. It was, as *The Forward*'s editor J.J. Goldberg memorably wrote on the centenary of the massacre,

> an act of violence that changed the course of Jewish history. Provoked by a medieval blood libel, flashed around the globe by modern communications, Kishinev was the last pogrom of the Middle Ages and the first atrocity of the twentieth century. The event, and the worldwide wave of Jewish outrage that it evoked, laid the foundations of modern Israel, gave birth to contemporary American-Jewish activism and helped bring about the downfall of the czarist regime.

Kishinev, then the capital of the Russian province of Bessarabia (and to contemporary Ukrainian Jewish jokesters, the little Moldovanaka sister of the Odessa Jewish neighbourhood made famous by the stories of Babel), is in modern times romanised as Chișinău in Moldova. Thus the city that produced the seminal event to have reshaped the history and demography of contemporary Ukrainian and Russian Jewry now lies outside of both. Though, since the airspace over Ukraine has been closed for the duration of the war, one still has to pass through there on every trip to nearby Odessa.

The Kishinev pogrom, the outcome of deep-seated divisions and resentments within the city, was incited by the antisemitic newspaper *Bessarabets* ("The Bessarabian"). Unsurprisingly, the paper was owned by the original publisher of the *The Protocols of the Elders of Zion* and had claimed that the Jewish citizens of the city had ritually murdered a local Russian boy for his blood. The Russian military garrison and local police did nothing to dispel the blood frenzy of the roving crowds. After the conclusion of the rioting, destruction and organised rape and murder committed by roving gangs, forty-nine Jews had been murdered and ten times that many had been wounded before the crowds dispersed. Religious Jewish women who had been raped were divorced by their weeping husbands.

The pogrom shaped the revolutionary consciousness for a generation of Zionist activists and leaders, including the young Ze'ev Jabotinsky – who was then a journalist living in Odessa. The pogrom, and the demeaning lack of reaction from the police and army, convinced many young Zionist leaders that Russian Jews needed to organise their own self-defence units to protect their themselves and their communities (thus the origins of Jabotinsky's infamous Revisionist Zionist slogan: "Jewish youth, learn to shoot!"). Another Odessan literary figure, the poet Chaim Nachman Bialik, also penned his epic Hebrew poem "In the City of Slaughter" after conducting several weeks of emotionally harrowing interviews with survivors of the pogrom. The great theme of his poem was servility and weakness; the immolation of the Jews who could do nothing to protect themselves from the clutches and depredations of the enraged mob. While it was infinitely more violent, the Kishinev pogrom proffered a foretaste of what would transpire next.

The extent of public antisemitism was highlighted by the great political scandal of the pre-revolutionary Russian Empire

The Beilis affair

It is important to understand the extent to which the memory of the savage anti-Jewish pogroms that took place across the Russian

Empire in the decades leading up to the 1917 revolution still haunts the collective psyche of post-Soviet and diaspora Jewry. The pogroms offered a continuous testament to how far Russia had fallen behind Western Europe in granting equal rights and protection to its Jewish citizens. The pogroms were also, ironically, the outcome of the riotous energies that terrified the tsarist government and which it had worked hard to contain. The extent of public antisemitism was highlighted by the great political scandal of the pre-revolutionary Russian Empire – the 1913 blood libel trial of Kyivan Jew Menachem Mendel Beilis.

In March 1911, Beilis, a perfectly assimilated night manager at a Kyiv brick factory, was accused of the ritual murder of a Ukrainian child whose body was discovered mutilated not far from Beilis's place of employment. He was tortured by the Russian police before spending two years in confinement awaiting trial. From the very start, it was obvious to everyone save the most fanatical antisemite that the prosecution possessed no real evidence. The principled detective of the Kyiv police force entrusted with investigating the case ultimately refused to work on it, and was eventually acquitted of accusations of professional misbehaviour by an imperial court. The proceedings featured numerous witness testimonies (including by non-Jewish experts) denying the existence of any Jewish rituals that included human blood sacrifice. A jury of ordinary Kyiv citizens quickly found the accused to be not guilty of all charges, even as elements of the imperial government coerced them to deliver a face-saving conviction.

The whole affair was a farce. In the words of American historian Steven Zipperstein in his excellent recent study of the Kishinev pogrom:

The accused was himself absurdly miscast: largely indifferent to Jewish ritual, he had served without complaint in the Russian army, befriended Russian neighbors who testified on his behalf at the trial, and made good friends of gentile prisoners that he had met in jail. Once found not guilty he became something of a local celebrity.

The exculpatory evidence in favour of Beilis, who always worked on the Sabbath, was based on his having accepted a delivery notice on the Saturday morning just as the murder was taking place.

Leon Trotsky – who was usually demure about his own Judaism – began his long and exasperated observation of the trial by noting that it was "one of those rare legal affairs which, notwithstanding their complete insignificance in terms of their starting point, turn into historical events which sear themselves into the consciousness of a country and, not infrequently, form a watershed between two chapters of its political life". The revolutionary believed the trial to have been part of the tsarist government's campaign to foment hatred of the Jews. Yet it was more complex: much like the Kishinev pogrom, the trial was a regional phenomenon that came to the capital. Several intellectuals and tsarist officials thought that antisemitism could serve as an ideological glue, holding Russia together in the face of the collapse of the legitimacy of the feeble Tsar Nicholas II – a sort of alternative ideology of hate that might stave off the decline of the empire.

The case demonstrated that swathes of the still broadly uneducated and illiterate population of the Russian Empire continued to believe in the worst sorts of medieval superstitions. That the epochal legal case of the Russian Empire's final years took place in Kyiv rather than Moscow or St Petersburg was significant – but also not surprising, as the Jewish populations of those cities were still marginal at the time. The affair had the effect of mobilising the Black Hundreds – ultra-monarchist, revanchist and jingoistic reactionaries – against the Russian Empire's Jewish subjects. A torrent of antisemitic libel swept through the Russian press, further destabilising the situation of Jewry across the teetering Russian Empire.

The Beilis affair is often described as the Russian version of the Dreyfus affair, which led the French to reckon with their relationship to their Jewish co-citizens. Except the Russian case was somehow – if possible – even more sinister, vulgar and debasing to all involved. It trumpeted the nasty antisemitism of the imperial Russian state across the pages of world newspapers. For his part, Beilis emerged as a precarious and somewhat pathetic figure. He steadfastly refused to take advantage of the moneymaking potential of his newfound celebrity and absconded from the Russian Empire for Palestine, eventually succumbing to an early death in America. As well as mobilising the antisemites, the affair energised and united many of the conflicting Jewish political movements of the time – from the Bundists to competing factions of Jewish socialists, integrationists, revolutionaries and proponents of emigration. It also left a mark – however unhappy – in literature, via Bernard Malamud's feisty Pulitzer Prize–winning novel *The Fixer* (1966).

Revolutionary times

The Beilis affair can be seen as a preamble for the ensuing tumult. The revolutionary, post-revolutionary and civil war periods in Ukraine were ones of tremendous excitement – as well as of violent carnage for the Jewry of the Russian Empire, most of whom were by this time concentrated in Poland and Ukraine. Jews embraced various modern political ideologies – often in order to leave the shtetl and become fully-fledged members of the society. Some embraced socialism. Others took up the banner of Communism or Zionism or the flagrantly anti-Zionist localism of the Bund, or various other utopian schemes. Hundreds of thousands chose to migrate to America (the correct answer from the standpoint of surviving the next hundred years, but perhaps the wrong one from the standpoint of holding onto their Yiddishkeit).

Vast libraries have been published on the topic of the Jews and the Bolshevik Revolution – and untangling which of the major early communists and revolutionaries should be classified as "Ukrainian Jews" rather than "Russian Jews" or "Soviet Jews" is a pleasant enough parlour game to while away an evening. Of course, though the revolution was not made by "the Jews", numerous revolutionary leaders were Jewish. The security and intelligence services were full of them and remained so until the dissolution of the Soviet Union. The communist revolution promised the Jews full emancipation – from both the strictures of traditional life administered by Russian-appointed rabbis and the repression by the tsarist regime. It was a revolutionary promise of full and equal citizenship as Soviet men and women. Many Jews eagerly took up the deal (including my own communist apparatchik, nomenklatura and commissar ancestors), whose price was the forced rejection of their religiosity, culture and most aspects of their Jewish particularism.

It was the Communist Party in Moscow that decreed the closure of every working synagogue across Ukraine

But the collapse of the Russian Empire did not bring relief to its Jewish subjects. Savage pogroms took place against the Jews immediately after the revolution – in towns such as Zhytomyr, Berdychiv and Korsun, as well as in Kyiv suburbs such as Hostomel and Bucha (which, a hundred years later, regained historical notoriety as the place where Russians troops committed atrocities during last spring's Battle of Kyiv). These gruesome deeds were carried out by roving military formations ranging from criminal gangs to organised armies, often filled with fighters who believed that Bolshevism was a Jewish creation. The pogroms continued as the empire was dissolving and its massive lands were falling into self-governing fiefdoms and short-lived states, until the Red Army gradually consolidated its control over formerly imperial territory spanning a dozen or so time zones.

The Ukrainian Central Rada, or parliament, founded in 1917 as part of the creation of an autonomous Ukrainian People's Republic, was brimming with Jewish political parties. These parties, which included Zionists, the diaspora nationalist Folkspartei, the moderate Faraynigte and the Jewish socialist Bund and Poale-Zion, usually had either antagonistic or symbiotic relationships with Ukrainian political parties. The majority of the Ukrainian parties in the Central Rada were socialist, and their ideologically equivalent Jewish parties would join them in ever-shifting alliances. On a few remarkable occasions the well-bred sons of prosperous Jewish merchants – such as Arnold Margolin – became deeply involved in the Ukrainian national independence politics of the era. As historian Seth Abramson writes,

> The experience of Ukrainian Jewry from 1917 to 1920 is a paradox in modern Jewish history. At the same moment that the leaders of the Ukrainian revolutionary movement extended unprecedented civil rights to Ukrainian Jews, pogromists operating in the name

of that same movement brutally terrorized hundreds of Jewish communities with violence and robbery.

Nonetheless, 1918 saw the blossoming in Kyiv – rather than in Petrograd or Moscow – of one of the most original artistic movements of Soviet Jewish culture of the last hundred years: the radical and radically secularist *Kultur Lige* art movement. The *Kultur Lige* incorporated modernist innovations into thrilling Yiddish-language theatre, literature, art and design. The artist El Lissitzky was a progenitor of the movement, whose abstract designs and typographical innovations became part of the wider legacy of the Russian avant garde. This revolutionary, aesthetically fresh movement strove to bring secular Yiddish art to the masses, and would be incredibly influential in modern and Jewish art – in the realms of book illustration and theatre especially. The movement spread to Latvia and Poland, but in Ukraine it was quickly quashed by the communists. Vladimir Lenin's Yevsektsiya (literally the "Jewish Section" of the party) – essentially executed a hostile takeover of the previously anarchic arts movement a mere two years after it was founded.

And it was the Communist Party in Moscow that decreed the closure of every working synagogue across Ukraine. The houses of worship were desacralised and (almost mockingly) put to other uses, from sports clubs to storage sheds. "None of this was initiated in Ukraine, whose Communist Party and government were completely subordinated to Moscow," states the recent historical narrative of Ukrainian Jewry during the war compiled by the Babyn Yar Memorial Foundation. "Overall," the report damningly concludes, "the Jewish proletarian organizations founded by the Yevsektsii and the Soviet authorities destroyed more than they created. And then the authorities liquidated them as well."

The Holodomor

In 1932–1933, Stalin artificially induced a famine in Soviet Ukraine. The agenda was both to export wheat to the West in exchange for desperately needed hard currency, and to break the recalcitrant Ukrainian farmers and broader Ukrainian nation. The famine, now known as the Holodomor, starved to death between 4 and 7 million Ukrainians (the numbers are still being debated) and inflicted psychic trauma on the Ukrainian nation for the next eighty years.

The tragedies of the Ukrainians and their Jewish neighbours were intimately intertwined. Hitler was cementing his power in Germany in January 1933, at the exact time the Ukrainians were being starved. Hundreds of thousands of Ukrainians Jews are estimated to have died along with their Ukrainian neighbours – starvation, of course, makes no distinction between faiths or ethnicities. The famine caused tremendous population movement and depopulation of the countryside: whoever possessed the strength rushed from their villages into the towns and cities. Jews likewise migrated en masse out of the shtetls, which were by that point overpopulated and desperately lacking in food and resources. The Holodomor, I believe, should be considered a Jewish tragedy as well as a Ukrainian one.

Ukrainians have spent the several decades since their independence lobbying to have their tragedy acknowledged by the international community – and particularly Israel – as an instance of premeditated ethnic genocide. That acknowledgement by Israel was the main request issued to Israeli prime minister Benjamin Netanyahu during his August 2019 election season visit to Kyiv. Some Israelis and other Diaspora Jews have seen the desire to claim genocide against other peoples in the twentieth century (such as the Armenians and Ukrainians) as a contravention of the unique historical status of the Holocaust. It is a position that has elicited criticism and some amount of resentment.

In the analysis of the American scholar Victoria Khiterer, the widespread Ukrainian suffering of the Holodomor was instrumental in conditioning Ukrainian tolerance for the horrors that came next. "If not for the Holodomor in Ukraine and Stalin's repressions of the 1930s," Khiterer writes,

> the attitude of the Kyiv gentile population toward the Holocaust would perhaps have been different. People had gotten so used to the suffering of others, victims of the famine and political repression, that they remained mainly passive, silent, and indifferent toward the mass execution of Jews [in the Babyn Yar massacre] during the Holocaust.

Unlike in Poland, the Nazis would not be successful in wiping away Jewish culture in Ukraine *tout court*, but they would be successful in transplanting what was left of Yiddish culture and the Hasidim to Brooklyn, Antwerp and Jerusalem.

The Holocaust and collaboration

Up to a million and a half Jews – about 60 per cent of Ukraine's pre-war population of 2.7 million – were killed throughout Ukrainian territory over the course of World War II. While most of those murders were carried out by Wehrmacht forces, they were in various towns assisted by Ukrainian police collaborators recruited from the local population.

The annihilation of the Jews of Eastern Europe – that is, the Jews in areas seized from the Soviet Union – is now known as the "Holocaust by bullets". Unlike in Western Europe, where Jewish deaths were mechanised through organised transportation to extermination camps and the innovative use of industrial methods, in Ukraine they would simply be methodically shot in town after town. Most of the Jews killed in Ukraine were shot within days of the Nazis taking over their villages and cities.

The question of Ukrainian culpability and victimhood in the Holocaust is complex. It is also the topic within the 2000-year history of Jewish life in these lands that brings out the strongest emotions – especially within Jewish diasporas outside Eastern Europe. Some Ukrainians were indubitably involved in committing crimes against Jews during the war, but the Ukrainian nation as a whole lacked self-rule and was occupied by the Soviets and the Nazis. At the same time, millions of Ukrainians also fought the Nazis, serving in the Red Army, as well as in Soviet and Polish partisan units.

The Soviet Union and Nazi Germany invaded Poland in a coordinated and perfidious assault in September 1939, partitioning the country and allowing the Soviets to annex the western Ukrainian provinces from the Polish state. For the next two years, these provinces were integrated into the Ukrainian Soviet Socialist Republic, including forced Russification and communisation that led to hatred of Moscow by the local citizenry. The German invasion of the Soviet Union on 22 June 1941 caught the Soviet authorities by surprise (though historians now inform us that it should not have). Resenting the Soviet authorities, many Ukrainian nationalists viewed the German invasion as an opportunity for autonomy; some of the older generation especially had fond or civilised memories of the Germans from World War I. The Soviets retreated in haste.

The representatives of the Organization of Ukrainian Nationalists (OUN), who had made common cause with the Nazis, entered

Lviv with them and seized the opportunity to declare their own independent state on German-occupied territory. The Ukrainian nationalists thought they would receive a deal on self-rule akin to the one the Nazis had offered the Croatians. The Germans quickly disabused them of such delusions. By August of that year, they had integrated Galicia into their Polish occupation administrative unit and given over swathes of the southern areas over to Romanian dominion (including the Dniester areas and the Odessa region of my family), with the rest of the country being declared the Ukrainian Reichskommissariat.

Before retreating from those territories, the Soviet Secret Service (NKVD) – the precursor to the KGB – committed mass executions in many Soviet prisons. In Lviv, the Red Army carried out what is now referred to as "the 1941 NKVD Prison Massacre", killing between 10,000 and 40,000 prisoners. This further enraged the Ukrainian population, which greeted the Nazi army streaming into the city as liberators – with flowers, music and dancing. The local Jewish population was swiftly blamed for the massacres in the Lviv prisons. In the weeks that followed, locals and members of the OUN engaged in a three-day pogrom of organised atrocities against the Jewish population of the city, killing and raping thousands. The German Einsatzgruppen – mobile death squads – organised another massacre of the remaining Jews of the city three weeks later as they began to plan the Holocaust on Ukrainian territory. The collaboration of the Ukrainian independence movement with Nazism involved connections between the two that began in the 1930s and included OUN members serving in auxiliary police units under German command from 1941 to 1943. Tragically, this tremendous moral error, which modern Ukraine needs to reckon with, has been exploited by its present-day opponents in Moscow to justify their own ongoing calamitous error.

Ideologically, the OUN were radical nationalist antisemitic integralists. The organisation had emerged after the Poles took over territory from the Austro-Hungarian Empire and moved to squelch the rights to autonomous education for the Ukrainian minority in their midst in an attempt to Polonise them. The more militantly radical wing of the OUN – the OUN-B – was led by Stepan Bandera, who spent most of the war interned in a Nazi camp, and believed in achieving its ends through violent and terrorist methods. By the autumn of 1942 the OUN-B had formed the Ukrainian Insurgent Army, which had strained, complex and antagonistic relations with the Germans but nonetheless concentrated on fighting the Bolsheviks and Soviet partisans (and continued doing so well into the 1950s, long after the vanquishing of the Nazis). Tens of thousands collaborated with the Nazis (though some did so to gain training and weapons which they later turned on the Nazis). By 1943–1944 they were engaging in combat with and large-scale ethnic cleansing of Poles in Volhynia and Eastern Galicia to prompt what they feared to be the re-establishment of the pre-war Polish borders.

In the meantime, the Nazis were attempting to eliminate Ukrainian Jewry. The main organised killings took place in Babyn Yar, which was then a ravine several kilometres outside Kyiv and is now located in the north of the sprawling city. The Nazis had already carried out massacres of this sort in the previous weeks as they took over territory in western Ukraine – about 23,600 Jews at Kamianets-Podilskyi were murdered over three days in late August 1941 – but Babyn Yar would constitute a blueprint for what would take place across the rest of the country, and in Belarus and the occupied Baltics. Over the course of two days – 29–30 September

1941 – around 34,000 Kyiv Jews were rounded up, marched to the ravine and shot by machine guns. Over the next several years, around 100,000 victims – the vast majority of them Jewish – were murdered at this site. Babyn Yar was also a place for the mass murder of Soviet POWs, some Ukrainian nationalists, Romani and others, and is rightly seen as a national site of trauma. The Nazis also emptied out the neighbouring psychiatric ward and executed its population at the killing site.

Babyn Yar eventually became the symbol of the methodical killing of Jews across the Soviet space – even though the Soviets had first allowed the site to be used as a garbage dump after the war. In the mid-1970s the Soviets permitted a brutalist monument to be erected, but it spoke obliquely of "Soviet citizens" rather than of Jewish victims of Nazi ideology.

Kyiv Jewry did not have the chance to erect a proper sculpture – the famous menorah – until autumn 1991, in a rare moment of consensus about what could be placed there. "No monument stands over Babi Yar," the rockstar Russian poet Yevgeny Yevtushenko began his epic poem in 1961. "A steep cliff only, like the rudest headstone./ I am afraid/ Today, I am as old/ As the entire Jewish race itself."

> *Maths departments would routinely give Jewish students unsolvable problems as part of their entry examinations*

Repression and refuseniks

The post-war period saw the systemisation of state antisemitism by the communists. A campaign was launched against so-called "rootless cosmopolitans" – that is, Jewish intellectuals – who were accused of being disloyal to the Soviet state (thus creating the modern script for accusations of dual loyalty). The campaign culminated with the "Doctors' plot" – when between 1951 and 1953 several prominent and mostly Jewish doctors were accused of conspiring to kill various leaders and Communist Party officials.

During the second half of the Soviet Union's existence, state antisemitism and its corollary – mandatory anti-Zionism – broke the promise of emancipation and equality that had been offered by the communist revolution. Jews were put under informal quota systems for admission to the best universities. Maths departments would routinely give Jewish students unsolvable problems as part of their entry examinations. Jewish students from Minsk to Moscow to Baku had to become adept at figuring out which universities they could attend – many were technical colleges on the periphery of the empire and in Ukraine. As late as 1983, during the final days of the Brezhnev era and right up to the days of Perestroika, my own aunt decided to change her name from her father's Jewish patronymic, Ruderman, to her mother's Russian surname, Seriabrikova, on her passport to gain acceptance into Moscow State University – the most prestigious university in the Soviet Union (she got in, dear reader). Soviet Jews found it almost impossible to advance to the highest levels of power. There were some exceptions: my mother's uncle Yuri Izrael, for example, the chairman of the Soviet Committee for Hydrometeorology between 1975 and 1991, wound up in charge of the Chernobyl clean-up – and, despite that surname, almost made it into the Politburo in the late 1970s and 1980s.

The Soviets repressed Jewish life, religion and culture. The activist Jewish resistance to this repression should be viewed as part of the wider resistance of minority nations (the Balts especially) that ultimately brought about the collapse of the Soviet project.

Sovietisation – with Russian as the imperial language binding together Soviet citizens – effaced minority cultures, which brought together the Ukrainian and Jewish peoples in symmetrical and often complementary repression. The refusenik movement was a serious response, and it engendered a remarkable Ukrainian–Jewish dialogue – conversations between Ukrainian nationalists and Jewish refuseniks that took place inside the Soviet Gulag system.

One of my proudest movements as the editor of an English-language literary magazine about Ukrainian culture after the Maidan Revolution was commissioning the British-Ukrainian writer, activist and former United Nations official Bohdan Nahaylo to pen an essay on this little-known historical moment. "In the post-Stalin era Ukrainians who had been accused of 'nationalism' consistently formed the largest group of political prisoners within the USSR," Nahaylo wrote.

In the 1950s Jewish inmates of the Gulag witnessed the remarkable resilience of the [Ukrainian Insurgent Army] veterans and representatives of the clergy and hierarchy of the Ukrainian Catholic Church ... Contrary to Soviet propaganda, they did not encounter Ukrainian anti-Semites, Holocaust deniers, or apologists for the Nazis. The Jews found that they had no problems getting on with them. And in the 1960s and 1970s the next generation of Soviet dissenters who ended up in the Gulag also quickly discovered that the anti-Ukrainian nationalist and anti-Jewish/Zionist myths being generated by the Soviet regime, aimed in no small part at sustaining enmity between the two peoples, did not hold up in frank and open discussions. Such open dialogue between the Ukrainian and Jewish political prisoners would never have been possible outside of the Zone (Gulag).

Jews were banned from leaving the Soviet Union, along with most other Soviet citizens (who might get to visit Cuba or the Warsaw Pact nations at best). The number of Jews who desired to flee the Soviet workers' paradise radically increased in the wake of the 1967 Six-Day War. The stunning Israeli victory stirred the activist class among Soviet Jewry to begin to campaign for their own rights. Sixteen idealistic young refuseniks – including two of their friends who were not Jewish – hatched a plot to hijack an airplane in a scheme to fly to Sweden. They were caught and fiercely prosecuted, being issued death sentences that were later rescinded. The lurid nationwide newspaper accounts of the caper both crystalised and popularised the refusenik movement.

The Soviet human rights and Jewish immigration movements intertwined at various points – including around figures such as Natan Sharansky and Andrei Sakharov as well as in the leadership and membership of the Helsinki group. Ukraine, it should be noted, was not much of a hotbed of Zionist activist opposition to the ban on Jewish emigration, though some cities – Kyiv and Chernowitz (where the prominent Yosyf Zisels grew up) – produced important movement leaders and future Israeli politicians, including Sharansky, who was from Donetsk.

The 1970s campaign by Jews outside the Soviet Union to demand the right of Soviet Jewry to emigrate eventually succeeded. Bowing to international pressure, Moscow allowed the emigration, which turned from a trickle into a flood over the course of the 1970s and into the '80s.

After the Soviet Union

By the time the Soviet Union had dissolved in 1991, the bulk of

Ukrainian Jewry – much like their coreligionists throughout the Soviet Union – had been forcibly transformed into secular citizens of the workers' paradise. Almost four generations of concerted repression of knowledge, traditions, culture and language had wiped away Soviet Jewish communal and institutional memory. Much of what could be passed along to the next generation, and tether Ukrainian, Russian and Belarusian Jews to their ancestors, was gone. In practice, even the most committed and fiery refusenik and Zionist activists had relatively little authentic Jewish knowledge or cultural capital to hold onto. Likewise, the swift collapse of the Soviet civilisational structures – an entire system of economic, political and social practices – was deeply disorienting and traumatic for those who had lived their whole lives under it.

Missionaries from every religion, sect and cult imaginable arrived in the post-Soviet world to fish for souls

Understandably, the Zionist activists began to leave for Israel as soon as their crusade succeeded and the doors of the Soviet Union swung open. Though a minuscule proportion of the total Jewish population of the USSR, they constituted a natural class of leaders, and their departure depleted the Jewish population of some its most energetic and vivacious personalities. In fact, the population of many post-Soviet states – including their Jewish communities – fell dramatically in the 1990s. Millions of Soviet Jews emigrated from across the Soviet Union's successor states to Israel, America, Europe and beyond. Ukraine's Jewish population continued to decrease precipitously throughout the 1990s and early 2000s. While the Jewish population of cities such as Dnipro, Kyiv, Donetsk and Kharkiv remained stable or grew, the Jewish communities of secondary cities such as Chernowitz contracted sharply – as did the existence of Yiddish as a living language. Today, if one hears a Jewish tongue spoken randomly in the streets of Ukrainian cities, it is Hebrew being spoken by repatriated Ukrainian Israelis or Israeli tourists.

Nationalism and revolution

The Ukrainian vote for independence on 1 December 1991 was in many ways the moment that concluded the Soviet project. Yet the 1990s were a chaotic and disorienting time. Hundreds of millions of people throughout the former Soviet Union were searching for spiritual taxonomies to fill yawning psychological gaps left by the collapse of Communism. These were, after all, deeply traumatised societies. In the early 1990s, missionaries from every religion, church, sect, millenarian or apocalyptic cult imaginable arrived in the post-Soviet world to fish for souls. Thus the revitalisation of Ukrainian Jewish life resembled the revival of other religions – it was anarchic, intense, random and often marked by the pedantic formalism and fanaticism of the newly observant. The Jewish revival in particular was broad and messy, and involved – ironically – representatives of the strictest Orthodox organisations leading mostly secular Jewish communities. The revival was abetted by tremendous injections of money from Western and North American Jewish organisations, though the most stridently traditional streams of Orthodoxy quickly won out – let us turn to a business metaphor – in the competition for market share of newly observant Jews.

While the Nazis had eviscerated Jewish life in Poland, a great deal of institutional matter and memory remained in Central European nations such as the Czech Republic, Romania and Hungary. In Central European nations where Communism had reigned for a shorter period or where the communist authorities were not totally successful in rooting out institutional and familial Jewish life, the post-communist Jewish revival did not always possess the same frenetic edge of neo-Orthodox rigour. In Ukrainian- and Russian-speaking regions across Ukraine, Belarus and Russia, Hasidic rabbis – usually emissaries from Chabad – took the lead in rebuilding local communities, as well as the institutional structures and businesses needed to maintain them. The mostly American and Israeli rabbis who settled in Ukraine were often descendants of Hasidic rabbis from these same lands, and unlike the representatives of more liberal streams of Judaism were often willing to build their lives in Ukraine. I now routinely meet across the world bright, Russian-speaking young rabbis whose fathers settled in post-Soviet nations. Like their Russian counterparts, Ukrainian Jews are still mostly secular – and their rabbis are mostly black-hat Orthodox Hasidim.

In November 2013, the Maidan Revolution of Dignity commenced in response to Moscow's demands (and bribes) for Kyiv to withdraw from a mostly symbolic free trade treaty with the European Union. The driving impulse behind the revolution was the corruption that had plagued the country for two decades. The kleptocratic government of Donbas boss Viktor Yanukovych had come to power in 2010 and pilfered an estimated year's worth of the Ukrainian GDP over the next two and half years. The revolution lasted until 22 February 2014, when President Yanukovych fled to Russia and the Maidan protestors broke into his palatial mansion and played with the ostriches in his private zoo. His own parliamentarians switched sides to vote his government out.

The revolution rocked the country out of its lethargic stupor and supercharged civil society and activism. Various rabbis and Jewish Ukrainian elites in Kyiv sided with the protestors, speaking out against the government. Young Jewish activists were visibly present at the protests, including Jewish Ukrainian Israeli Defense Forces veterans who would drill their fellow protestors in the military skills needed to fend off the security services' attacks. Many of these Ukrainian Israelis found prominent roles in Ukrainian politics and civil society over the next decade. From 2014 to 2019, the Ukrainian parliament had a pair of fluent Hebrew speakers, including one who renounced his Israeli passport to take up his role.

The Maidan both created the modern Ukrainian political nation and served as the rebirth of an old one. In the early months after the Maidan, some antisemitic incidents took place in Kyiv and elsewhere, including the fire-bombing of a synagogue and the vandalising of a Holocaust memorial. Yet the participation of large numbers of Jewish activists and communal leaders in the Maidan did not go unnoticed. Ukrainian Jewry earned the status of insiders in the new national story. This was a civic revolution and it embraced anyone who wanted to be part of it. Polling indicated that Ukraine was now by far the least antisemitic and least bigoted country in Eastern Europe. The new Ukrainian civic national identity enshrined European values and aspirations into the social compact (and European Union and NATO candidate status into the constitution).

At the same time, the Kremlin viewed even the slightest sort of integration of Ukraine into Western economic, political and social institutions as a direct threat to its capacity to continue dominating the country, as it had done for two decades via proxies and gas contracts. An independent and sovereign Ukraine not dominated by bribable and malleable kleptocrats or Moscow proxies threatened the Russian regime, and Ukrainian democracy led to autocratic fears of what political scientists refer to as democracy contagion. Putin, who had exhibited an obsession with Ukraine, began pushing back against Ukrainian attempts at democratic and clean self-governance.

Putin's Ukraine obsession

Less than a week after the conclusion of the Maidan Revolution, Putin informed his generals to begin the process of "returning" Crimea back to Russia. He sent masses of troops wearing no military insignia or markings (these became known as the "little green men") to take over strategic sites and government buildings in the Crimean Peninsula. The outgunned Ukrainian military units, receiving no coherent orders from Kyiv, stood down. The Russian Federation annexed the peninsula in March, thus beginning the war against Ukraine. Russian television propaganda blared out the patently ridiculous statement that Crimean Jews were finally free to celebrate Passover under their protection. Russian special forces began to infiltrate the eastern Donbas regions, taking over city halls and military installations as Putin decided to break the Ukrainian political project and split the country in half.

It was the first time in a century that large Jewish communities in two European nations found themselves at war

The war sundered Jewish communal links between the occupied zones and the rest of the country. This also led to a political rupture within Chabad as numerous rabbis had kin split between communities – especially in Crimea. Eventually a meeting had to be arranged in the Brooklyn headquarters of the movement to smooth over relations between emissaries who'd been forced by political realities to take partisan positions on the conflict (something they typically prefer not to do) while tending to flocks in Russia and Ukraine. The Jewish communities of the cities of Donetsk and Luhansk were evacuated as rabbis and leaders took most able-bodied adults out of the region. For the first time since the end of World War II, tens of thousands of Jews had to flee. It was also the first time in a century that large Jewish communities in two European nations found themselves at war, with the corollary necessity of having to prove their patriotic bonafides to their countrymen. Perhaps even more than average Ukrainians – many of whom have family in Russia – Ukrainian Jews remain connected to their Russian Jewish brethren by family ties.

The Ukrainian parliament elected in the 2014 elections was likely the most Jewish of any Eastern European nation in half a century. Ukrainian Jewish elites who made informal counts privately informed me that openly or discreetly Jewish members of parliament constituted at least 15 per cent of its 450 members. Intriguingly, unlike the politics of a century ago, which produced numerous Jewish socialist parties, contemporary Jewish representation was spread across every party represented in the Rada – from the western Ukrainian centre-right nationalist Samopomosh "Self Help" party to the pro-Moscow fifth columnists in the Opposition Platform and Poroshenko's European Solidarity party. He embraced a brand of nationalism that promoted Ukrainian language and culture as early as 2014, and, after coming to power, Poroshenko was deeply philosemitic and had close ties to Jewish elites. In 2016, Volodymyr Groysman – a Jewish politician – ascended to the prime minister's chair under the tutelage of Poroshenko. Poroshenko also made a serious push to complete negotiations on a free trade accord with Israel in the run-up to Ukraine's presidential elections of 2019. (Incidentally, the countless Western newspaper headlines proclaiming that Groysman was "the first Jewish prime minister of Ukraine" were a pet peeve of mine at the time. Yukhym Zvyahilsky, who served as acting prime minister for less than a year in late 1993, was also Jewish.)

On the other hand, as the war with Russia continued, Poroshenko placed activist historians who held jingoistic and particular views of World War II and the role of fighters against the Soviet regime in charge of Ukrainian memory policy. These historians valorised the role of Ukrainian nationalists whose movements were complicit in the ethnic cleansing of Jews and Poles. This sort of thing supported Russian propaganda and appeared to contradict Poroshenko's excellent ties with the Jewish community (many of whom shrugged such politics away).

These contradictions remained unresolved over the next five years. Many Ukrainian Jews were ambivalent about the official distortion of history; the country had embraced them, and the governments of Ukraine and Russia were essentially in the middle of public arguments about who loved their Jews more.

The rise of Zelensky

As in Russia, Jewish businessmen had an outsized presence in the new class of rapacious businessmen who had captured the Ukrainian state. One, Victor Pinchuk, had married the daughter of a president. Another, Igor Kolomoysky, was one of the most prominent and wealthy oligarchs – and certainly the most buccaneering. A hilariously profane bad-boy figure, Kolomoysky was appointed governor of Dnipropetrovsk Oblast by Poroshenko when eastern Ukraine began to look as if it could fall under Russian dominion. Kolomoysky's mandate was to keep this from happening. He personally bankrolled a pair of battalions and placed substantive bounties on the heads of separatist leaders. Suspected separatists, saboteurs and Russian proxy troops were reported to have disappeared in the woods under his watch. Appointing the carnivalesque Kolomoysky, who kept an aquarium full of sharks in his Dnipro office, was a political stroke of genius and his brutish actions in those early days of the war were critical to keeping the Dnipro region from being overrun by the Russian proxy collaborators.

Flush with his feelings of success, Kolomoysky – essentially a warlord in a time of limited state capacity – went on to massively overplay his hand when he ordered detachments of his heavily armed and balaclava-clad personal army to engage in business-related vendettas back in Kyiv. He ordered them to seize control of the offices of the state oil company in the spring of 2015. The armed men did not allow the newly appointed CEO of the state oil agency to enter the building and began to raise an iron fence around it. Poroshenko delivered an ultimatum – government troops would take the building by force if Kolomoysky did not back down. Faced with a firefight, the oligarch folded and duly appeared in the presidential offices around midnight, where Poroshenko chastised and humiliated him in front of the cameras and sacked him from his post as wartime governor. Kolomoysky fled to Switzerland, where he waited for an opportunity to settle scores with his nemesis. The opportunity to do so emerged four years later, with the chance to back the unlikely presidential campaign of a Jewish comedian.

Volodymyr Zelensky was a handsome, sprightly and successful show business executive and comedian from the south-eastern Russian-speaking part of Ukraine who had co-founded the Kvartal 95 production studio with a tightknit group of childhood pals. Zelensky had tap-danced his way to success in broad and lowbrow comedy skits (the aesthetic was 1980s Soviet popular humour, by way of Benny Hill) and had starred in romantic comedies. In 2015, Zelensky and his friends released a TV series, *Servant of the People*, in which he played an ordinary and decent Ukrainian history teacher propelled to power when a video of his expletive-laden rant about Ukrainian politicians is uploaded by a student. In the show, the video becomes a viral sensation, and the Ukrainian people vote the everyman hero into office with 67 per cent of the vote. In real life, the electorate gave him almost three-quarters of the vote.

Servant of the People aired on a Kolomoysky-owned television station and the presidential campaign was partly financed by the oligarch, some of whose people wound up on Zelensky's parliamentary party list during the election. But Zelenksy came to power repudiating the oligarchy, just as his everyman character had done in the show. Upon being sworn in, he was not terribly ideological;

Zelensky leaned into his Jewish identity for the greater good of the country

his instincts were moderate and liberal. But the learning curve of a presidency in an anarchic country with a brutal political environment is steep. The initial results of the Zelensky presidency were decidedly mixed, especially after he – unluckily – tried to reboot his cabinet with a reshuffle in the first weeks of the Covid pandemic. He also become a side character in Donald Trump's first impeachment, which examined the US president's alleged efforts to pressure Zelensky to investigate Joe Biden's son.

Having met Zelensky before his presidential campaign, I am routinely asked about my assessment of his character. "Ukrainians voted for a mixture of Benny Hill and Boris Johnson," I typically say, "and they somehow wound up with Churchill."

The war

The Russian assault on Kyiv on 24 February was meant to decapitate the Ukrainian government within three days. Western intelligence agencies and the Kremlin both assumed that the capital would fall and that the government would flee. This, clearly, did not happen. Instead, Zelensky refused an American offer to leave the capital (whether he ever actually uttered the immortal words "I need ammunition, not a ride" will become known in time from the archives) and rallied the nation during the steadfast defence of the capital. His performance, as the entire world has since learned, was phenomenal and heroic.

While bombing the main Kyiv television tower in the north of Kyiv, the Russians hit the park at the edge of the ravine of the Babyn Yar memorial, killing two citizens. The symbolic aspects of this assault were obvious. Zelensky leaned into his Jewish identity for the greater good of the country. His becoming a wartime president and world historical statesman melded with his acceptance of his Jewish identity. It is not coincidental that Ukraine, in the midst of this war, has been led by Russian-speaking Ukrainians – many of them, such as defence minister Oleksii Reznikov and the mayor of Kyiv, Vitali Klitschko, of Jewish descent. The Russian accusations of the state being run by neo-Nazis appear all the more absurd when the commander-in-chief and many in the political class are Jewish. The Ukrainian nation has often engaged in revolts against its oppressors, but these were often doomed – especially when they represented a narrow ethnic Ukrainian identity that excluded, sometimes violently, Jews, Poles and other ethnic groups. Now, a new modern vision of Ukraine had emerged – a Ukraine whose ideals were liberal and democratic and inclusive of everyone who had been born on its soil.

Zelensky was a prime example of a generation of late-Soviet Jews who did not know what Jewish culture or tradition was. When I discussed the issue with him before he was president, he made some vague, proforma comments about Jews having always lived in Ukraine without issues. Zelensky was from a typically assimilated family and, having been exposed to limited Jewish education, had little understanding of Jewish life other than through the Holocaust, which had claimed many relatives of his uncle and other family. His Judaism, and what it means to be Jewish in his country, were not topics he was particularly comfortable with – until the war.

During one of his countless public addresses to national parliaments, Zelensky began to berate the Israeli Knesset for not doing enough in light of the genocide being experienced by Ukrainians. He also described Ukraine, facing a foe like neighbouring Russia, as a "big Israel" which would need to focus on security and self-defence.

The war has reshaped the territory, culture and politics of Ukraine for generations to come. At least a quarter – and perhaps as much as 40 per cent – of the Ukrainian pre-war population has been displaced. One of the less well-known stories of the war is the role of former Israeli special service operators who extracted untold numbers of at-risk individuals from the country, including elderly Holocaust survivors and those on Russian kill lists, be they Jews, evangelical Christians, Protestants or Jehovah's Witnesses.

An estimated 10 million Ukrainians took refuge in neighbouring European countries, though some have returned as the Ukrainian army has secured parts of the country. This number is thought to include at least half of all the Jews in Ukraine – though statistics are, as ever, impossible to come by. Adult men are not allowed to leave, but many have sent their families to other countries, such as Poland, Moldova, Israel and Germany. The Jewish communities in eastern

Ukraine have been emptied of all but the very elderly who do not wish – or are not able – to leave their homes. But some Ukrainian Jews who have fled their homes have been settling in the country's west, raising the prospect that communities may start to grow there for the first time in decades.

The future of Ukraine's Jews

When I attended the Passover Seder in Odessa last year – this was during the first two months of the war, when the city was still entrenched behind sandbags and anti-tank emplacements – only a quarter of the 200 or so people in the room were women.

The Seder took place the day after the Ukrainian navy had succeeded in sinking the *Moskva* – the warship flag carrier of the Russian Black Sea Fleet. The room was lit by candles after curfew so as not to give light signals to Russian bombers flying over the city. Everyone at the Seder, from the rabbi down, made the same jokes comparing Putin to Pharaoh: "So God opened up the Black Sea as if for Moses and the Russian warship was submerged in it." My own friends in Odessa were by this time sending their kids and grandmothers to Germany and Romania, understanding full well the irony of Romanians and Germans – who had slaughtered their grandparents and great-grandparents during the Holocaust – now providing succour to Odessan Jews. It was a total and surreal reversal. My Russophone friends and acquaintances began to send emails and texts to each other in Ukrainian, and the city council voted to take down its statue of Catherine the Great.

The war has, for the first time in a hundred years, put large numbers of European Jews at war with each another. It has reshaped and will continue to reshape the Jewish Diaspora, from Berlin to

London to New York City. Many pro-Putin Ukrainian Jewish and Russian Jewish oligarchs found that their previous game – living in opulence abroad off the benefits of stolen assets – was no longer tenable and wound up on sanctions lists with their assets frozen. Kolomoysky, who by this time was wanted and sanctioned by the Americans and under risk of a grand jury indictment, was even threatened with being stripped of his Ukrainian citizenship. Russophone Jewish communal life throughout the Diaspora was now disrupted, with Russian and Ukrainian Jewish ties fraying. Honourable – and not so honourable – Russian-born Israelis who had led international Jewish organisations for decades were being forced to step down because of their relationships – however close or informal – with Putin and the Russian state.

The long divorce between Russians and Ukrainians is mirrored by the schism between Ukrainian and Russian Jewish communities, as the two nations are set to evolve in different directions after the war. Putin, ironically, has done more to Ukrainianise the country with missile and rocket fire than anyone else in the decades since independence. Ukraine will certainly become more Ukrainian when the fighting finally ends.

Much like Ukraine, Ukrainian Jewry – a category that at its fullest expression incorporates legendary figures such as the Baal Shem Tov, Isaac Babel, Golda Meir and, now, Volodymyr Zelensky – will doubtless survive, and over the years even flourish. Yet the damage already wrought is monstrous, and this community has once again been scattered and disturbed due to the whims of a foreign power. We will be sifting through the ruins of a single psychotic megalomaniacal gamble for years to come.

The cover of the first issue of *The Jewish Quarterly*, Spring 1953

The Jewish Quarterly at seventy
David Herman

In 1974 there was a dinner in London to celebrate the twenty-first anniversary of *The Jewish Quarterly*. Its founding editor, Jacob Sonntag, spoke of what led him to found the journal:

> If I were asked how I envisaged *The Jewish Quarterly* when I started it more than twenty years ago, I would say that it was to cultivate literary journalism in the best tradition of Central and Eastern Europe and, in particular, in the best tradition of Eastern European Jewish writing ... I belong to the generation which looked for a synthesis between our Jewishness and our Europeanism.

These two worlds – the German-speaking literary culture of interwar Vienna and Prague, and the Jewish literary culture of Galicia, Bukovina and Eastern Europe – were Sonntag's cultural home and they are where the voice of the *Quarterly* came from.

Jacob Sonntag was born in 1905 at Vinnytsia in northern Bukovina, then part of the Austro-Hungarian Empire (now in Ukraine). Bukovina had been home to the Israeli writer Aharon Appelfeld, the great poet Paul Celan and novelist Gregor von Rezzori. There is a plaque in nearby Czernowitz that reads,

"Czernowitz, halfway between Kiev and Bukarest, Krakau and Odessa, was the secret capital of Europe ... where there were more bookshops than bakeries."

Sonntag's family moved to eastern Galicia and then to Austria during World War I – first to Innsbruck and then to Vienna. During the 1920s he wrote for German-language Jewish newspapers in Vienna. After the fascist coup in Austria in 1934, he moved to Czechoslovakia and, after the Germans invaded, he escaped to Britain in November 1938, where he resumed work as a freelancer, writing and translating for a number of Jewish publications in Britain. He founded *The Jewish Quarterly* in 1953, editing it from that year until his death in 1984.

This year marks the seventieth anniversary of the *Quarterly*. This is a good opportunity to introduce many new readers to the history of the journal and the story of how it began.

In 1953 the *Quarterly* was a very different publication from today. It was smaller than an old Penguin paperback, and you could buy a copy for half a crown. Open the first issue today and it seems almost impossibly remote. Take the opening article, by Jacob Fichman, born in Bessarabia in 1882. It had been originally published in Yiddish, in a Vilna-based journal, *Di Yiddishe Velt*, in 1928. Who would begin a new magazine with such an article? Then you start to read it. "It was many years ago, in Odessa," Fichman begins. "I was strolling along the beach with Bialik." Chaim Nachman Bialik, one of the great Yiddish and Hebrew poets, born in Volhynia in the Russian Pale, talks to the young Fichman about Mendele Sforim, the grandfather of Yiddish literature. Then you understand why Sonntag spoke so movingly about continuity: "We felt called upon to add a link to the 'golden chain'," he said, "handed to us by an earlier generation."

The *Quarterly* was founded in Britain by Jewish refugees from Central and Eastern Europe. The context was crucial. The early issues were marked by a strong sense of loss: not just of relatives who had been killed but of a whole vanished world of European Jewry. As Natasha Lehrer, still the literary editor of the *Quarterly*, wrote in her introduction to *The Golden Chain* (2003), published to celebrate the fiftieth anniversary of the journal, "The gaze of the *Quarterly* in the first three decades was turned eastwards, towards the ravaged European landscape of Sonntag's past."

What is surprising is that the magazine was not more elegiac

In an editor's note in 1973, Sonntag wrote:

> Let us recall the year 1953, the year *The Jewish Quarterly* was born. Less than a decade after the end of World War Two, its aftermath was felt but not truly comprehended. The Nazi holocaust made of all of us who were spared because "we were not there", survivors. It took some time for this awareness to grow as it took the actual survivors a long time to relate their experiences. Andre Schwarz-Bart's *The Last of the Just*, the first great epic to tell the story in a European language, had not yet been published (the original French edition came out in 1959, and the English edition only in 1961). It was only in 1953 that Reitlinger's *Final Solution* made its appearance (and Hilberg's *The Destruction of the Jews in Europe* followed only in 1961). The capture and trial of Eichmann had yet to take place.

It is not surprising to see, during the 1950s, a preoccupation with the Holocaust. After all, so many of the founding figures were refugees or, like Sonntag's wife, had lost their parents in the Holocaust. The first issues included reviews of Gerald Reitlinger's *The Attempt to Exterminate the Jews of Europe, 1939–1945*; essays such as Alexander Baron's "The Anniversary", published on the tenth anniversary of the beginning of the mass deportations of Jews from Paris; an interview with Louis Golding, the first Western European novelist to engage with the Warsaw Ghetto Uprising; translations of Holocaust poems in Yiddish and pieces on figures such as Janusz Korczak.

What is surprising is that the magazine was not more elegiac. Many of the articles about the destruction of European Jewry were thoughtful and detached. Compare them with the growing preoccupation with the Holocaust in the magazine in the 1980s and '90s. What explains this difference of tone? Of course, these pieces were written by survivors from Bukovina, Warsaw and Kraków. Many of these key figures in the early years of the magazine were too close to the experience of loss and displacement to be lachrymose. The emphasis was on recording what had happened.

The Holocaust was one crucial part of the context of the *Quarterly*. A second key part was that the magazine was founded right after the death of Stalin, just before the Rosenbergs were executed and a year after the Slansky trial. It was the height of the Cold War and many of the first issues addressed the cultural impact of Communism: the execution of the Yiddish writers by Stalin in 1952, the publication of Isaac Deutscher's biographies of Stalin (1949) and Trotsky (Volume 1, 1954).

But what truly set the *Quarterly* apart in its early years was its concern with language. What is the language of Jewish identity: Hebrew, Yiddish or English? Above all, there was a strong commitment to Yiddish writing, new translations of Yiddish poetry and a sense of "our great cultural heritage". This was decades before the late-twentieth-century revival of interest in Yiddish and in Eastern European Jewish culture, from klezmer to the translation of the great Jewish Soviet and Eastern European writers.

No other literary journal in the English-speaking world was so committed to preserving and transmitting the legacy of the great Yiddish writers of Eastern Europe and the Russian Pale. Its first issue features a piece by Sonntag called "Peretz Rediscovered", accompanied by translations of two poems, a story ("The Rabbi's Hat") and an extract from a dramatic poem ("The Golden Chain") by I.L. Peretz. Later in the issue there are poems by Yiddish poets such as Zalman Shneur and Eliezer Steinbarg, and an essay called "Plea for Yiddish". In the second issue there is a piece by Sonntag about the Yiddish poet Abraham Reisen, who had recently died. Sonntag called him "one of the last great names in modern Yiddish literature, representing a direct link with the great classical Yiddish writers of the nineteenth century and the beginning of this century". Note the word "link" and its echo of Peretz's "golden chain". These words illuminate a key aspect of Sonntag's vision for the magazine. It was a bridge thrown over an abyss, reaching out to Yiddish Europe's pre-war past.

In the editorial of the second issue, Sonntag puzzled over letters from some readers who "found that too much stress was laid on 'Yiddish' and not enough on 'Hebrew'". "To some," he wrote, "'Yiddish' seems to be synonymous with everything that they would like to eradicate and erase from their memories and consciousness." He was having none of this. With passion, he continued, "If continuity has any meaning, it can only mean to build on what preceding generations have created and handed on to us." We would be "foolish" to remove "all that which is valuable and has still a meaning for our own time. It is this, and not sentimental nostalgia, that moves us to try to preserve for our own time and generation some of the achievements of Yiddish culture."

And so the translations continued. In the third issue: poems by Leib Olitski and Abraham Sutzkever; in the fourth issue, three poems by Itzik Manger – like Sonntag a refugee born in Bukovina – and an essay on "The Cinderella of Languages". A few years later, the first anthology of writings from the *Quarterly* (*Caravan*, published in 1962) contained a section of Yiddish prose and verse, with poems by Peretz, Reisin and Manger and a story by Sholem Aleichem. And always there was the same sense of how precarious this legacy was. How little it was known. In a later anthology, *Jewish Perspectives: 25 Years of Jewish Writing* (1980), there is a small section on Soviet-Yiddish poetry with a short note by Sonntag. He ends, "Regrettably, very little of their work is available in English translations." Sonntag kept the flame burning. In mid-1950s Britain, a literary culture still dominated by T.S. Eliot and F.R. Leavis, to champion such poets, or even Yiddish itself, must have seemed quixotic, almost bizarre. It was one of the *Quarterly*'s greatest achievements.

But the *Quarterly* wasn't just focused on Yiddish and Eastern European literature. It was born at a crucial moment in the emergence of Anglo-Jewish culture in the mid-1950s, and was a fascinating synthesis of European Jewish literature and a new generation of Anglo-Jewish writers. From the beginning, the *Quarterly* defined itself as "an independent Anglo-Jewish cultural magazine".

The magazine championed a new generation of Jewish artists (David Bomberg, Lucian Freud, Frank Auerbach and Josef Herman), writers (Gerda Charles, Emanuel Litvinoff, Alexander Baron, Bernice Rubens, Frederic Raphael, Wolf Mankowitz and the poet Dannie Abse) and playwrights such as Harold Pinter and Arnold Wesker, most of whom were contributors to the *Quarterly* in its early years.

It is not surprising that Jacob Sonntag from Bukovina was interested in Yiddish and Hebrew literature; what was truly astonishing was that he was so open to the emerging Anglo-Jewish culture in the 1950s and '60s, which was being produced by the children of immigrants who had settled in the East End such as Baron and Wesker and refugee poets such as Michael Hamburger and Karen Gershon.

And, of course, there was the new state of Israel, founded in 1948. Chaim Weizmann died in 1952 and David Ben-Gurion resigned in 1953. From the beginning, the *Quarterly* engaged with debates about Israel and Israeli culture, including a special tenth-anniversary issue in 1958.

Swimming resolutely against the current, The Quarterly championed two developments neglected by the larger culture

In short, the *Quarterly* was founded at a moment of "immense changes". In his first editorial, Sonntag wrote, "British Jewry has emerged as the largest single Jewish Community in the whole of Europe (outside the Soviet Union) and as the fourth largest throughout the world (after the US, USSR and Israel)." "This geographical shift," he went on, "is of the greatest significance." What he was referring to, clearly, was not just the emergence of British Jewry but the near destruction of Central and Eastern European Jewry and its extraordinary culture by Nazism and Stalinism.

There were many absences too. There were few women contributors or subjects. And the magazine was very Eurocentric: it wasn't interested in the explosion of Jewish cultural energy in America. It contained nothing on Saul Bellow or Arthur Miller, even though *The Adventures of Augie March* and *The Crucible* both appeared in 1953, the year the *Quarterly* was first published. There was little on popular culture, hardly anything about film or television.

Perhaps more surprising was the absence of many of the Jewish refugees who made such a huge contribution to British culture in the 1940s and '50s: filmmakers such as Emeric Pressburger, Alexander Korda and Karel Reisz; historians, philosophers and critics such as Lewis Namier, Zara Steiner and Isaiah Berlin; scientists such as Bernard Katz, Hermann Bondi and Ernst Chain. It wasn't just that they didn't write for the *Quarterly*; they were rarely even mentioned. One explanation might be that the magazine became a home for outsiders – those who were less famous than insiders like Berlin, Namier and Korda (all of whom were knighted).

Finally, there was the absence of Sephardi culture. This was to change dramatically in the 1980s with the inclusion of writers and critics such as Moris Farhi and Gabriel Josipovici and historians of Salonica and the Jewish world of the Middle East.

This may sound like a lot of big gaps for a Jewish magazine: more holes than net. However, this misses its extraordinary achievement during these early years. Swimming resolutely against the current, the *Quarterly* passionately championed two developments that had been neglected by the larger culture. First and foremost, the Jewish culture of Eastern Europe in the half-century before it was destroyed by Hitler and Stalin. Second, the new generation of post-war Jewish writers in Britain.

What is striking about the first decade of the *Quarterly* was its sense of having one foot in the past and one in the present. It was the coming together of these two different groups that gave it its energy: refugees and immigrants from Central and Eastern

Europe, trying to preserve a lost world; and younger Anglo-Jewish writers, mostly the children and grandchildren of immigrants from Eastern Europe. For both groups the magazine was a literary home.

This synthesis continued through the 1960s and '70s. There was still the world of Soviet history and the Holocaust: Isaac Deutscher's "Memoirs of a Jewish Revolutionary" (1960); Isaac Babel's "The Beginning" (translated from Russian in 1962); Rafael Scharf's "Ringelblum of the Archives" (1980). This was coupled with the vanished world of Yiddish literature: S. An-ski's "The Trial: A Chassidic Folktale" (1964), Chimen Abramsky's "The 'Golden Age' of Soviet-Yiddish Literature that Was Brutally Destroyed" (1965); a tribute to Manger on his death (1969).

And, as ever, there was the other side of the *Quarterly*: Anglo-Jewish writing. Pieces such as Abse's "Ezra Pound and My Father" (1963), Litvinoff's famous poem "To T.S. Eliot" (1966), three scenes from Wesker's play *The Merchant* (1976). What is so interesting about these pieces is how they try to bring together the authors' sense of their own Jewish identity with the larger, dominant non-Jewish literary culture (Pound, Eliot and Shakespeare). It was the voice of outsiders.

In the mid-1980s came the great turning point. Jacob Sonntag died on 27 June 1984, after more than thirty years as editor. As historian W.D. Rubinstein wrote in the *Oxford Dictionary of National Biography*, "Sonntag edited the *Quarterly* almost single-handedly, always on a shoestring budget, and operating from his own home in north London." I still remember my last visit to his home in Worcester Crescent in NW7, full of books and papers, not a computer in sight – so similar to the homes of the Jewish scholar Chimen Abramsky and Leo Labedz, the founding editor of the journal *Survey*.

Sonntag's death was the beginning of the end of the close-knit group of contributors who wrote for the magazine during its first thirty years. By the 1980s they were almost all in their sixties and seventies. Few of the new contributors could read Yiddish, let alone remember the world of Bialik or Abraham Nahum Stencl, of Bukovina or interwar Warsaw, Prague and Vienna.

For Sonntag, the *Quarterly* was perhaps, above all, a textual homeland. Under his editorship the *Quarterly* was interested in art, history and ideas, certainly – but at its heart was language and literature. Yiddish and Hebrew, of course, but also the German of Central European modernism: Feuchtwanger, Kafka, Zweig, Max Brod and Nelly Sachs, all important subjects in the early issues.

*

It was time for a new generation of editors and contributors to reinvent the *Quarterly*. No more refugees, though there was a significant number of second-generation writers. Perhaps the best editor of the *Quarterly* after Sonntag was Matthew Reisz (1997–2007), son of the Czech-Jewish refugee filmmaker Karel Reisz. Through his father, Matthew had a lived connection with that Jewish, Central European world of the refugee generation.

In the years after Sonntag, three different groups emerged who had a huge impact on the new voice of the *Quarterly*. First, there was a group of prominent academics, from both sides of the Atlantic: Steven Beller ("Fin de Siècle Vienna and the Jews: The Dialectics of Assimilation", 1986), Saul Friedländer ("The Shoah between Memory and History", 1990), Mark Mazower ("Homage to Salonika, the Capital of Vanished Worlds", 1997). In its first thirty years, it was a magazine written by a small circle of outsiders, freelancers, novelists and journalists. Suddenly, the *Quarterly* had entered the mainstream of academic and intellectual debate at the very moment when Britain and America were opening up to Jewish culture and history.

Secondly, from the 1980s there was a new generation of Anglo-Jewish "Young Turks", critics and historians, including Bryan Cheyette, David Cesarani and David Feldman, who reassessed the central narratives and pieties of Anglo-Jewish history.

Finally, there was a new generation of British, American and Israeli writers including Aharon Appelfeld ("The Road to Myself", 1984), Clive Sinclair ("The El-Al Prawn", 1997), David Grossman ("Israel at Fifty", 1998), Linda Grant ("Delmore Schwartz and Me", 1999–2000), Howard Jacobson (*Vay Iz Mir* – Who'd Be a Jewish Writer?", 2001), Zadie Smith ("'The Limited Circle Is Pure': Kafka Versus the Novel", 2003), Etgar Keret ("Bad Karma", 2010) and Naomi Alderman ("Anne Frank and So On", 2012).

> *There is a new ambition, a new reach and new readers*

At last, there were more women contributors: Linda Grant, Zadie Smith, Naomi Alderman, Anne Karpf, Lisa Appignanesi, Eva Hoffman, Sonja Linden's essay on working with victims of torture and persecution. Above all, there was a breakthrough of young women editors and guest editors, Elena Lappin (1994–97), Rachel Lasserson (2007–13), Natasha Lehrer and Devorah Baum (guest editors of the fiftieth and sixtieth anniversary issues).

You can see the differences in the fiftieth anniversary anthology, *The Golden Chain: Fifty Years of The Jewish Quarterly*, edited by Natasha Lehrer in 2003. There is a clear shift from Yiddish-Soviet writing and Eastern Europe to contemporary Israel and America, from the Anglo-Jewish writing of the 1950s and '60s to a new generation at the turn of the century, the Sephardi world of Cairo and Salonika, female voices such as Sacha Rabinovitch lovingly recalled by her son Gabriel Josipovici, the American poet Adrienne Rich and poets such as Ruth Fainlight and Elaine Feinstein.

In 2013 there was a special double issue celebrating the sixtieth anniversary of the *Quarterly*, edited by Devorah Baum, a British literary critic who features in this very issue. Again, there were plenty of well-known figures: Simon Schama on making history, comedian David Baddiel, Martin Amis on the Jewish-American novel, Eva Hoffman and Lisa Appignanesi on writing about memory. The range of subjects is just as striking: from theology and popular culture to masculinity and psychoanalysis, from Isaiah Berlin to Stefan Zweig. The sense of the journey travelled since 1953 was perhaps best captured by a quotation from Larry David in Devorah Baum's editorial: "Religion doesn't play any part in my life in terms of how I live my life. But I don't think I've ever gone through a day in my life without hearing someone say the word 'Jew' or saying it myself."

The magazine covered more of the cultural waterfront. The big new books and films were reviewed, the major figures were appraised, the topical issues were discussed. But was there the same kind of centre? Was there a group of writers, either in English or in translation, who mattered in the same way as Yiddish poetry or Wesker mattered in the 1950s? The *Quarterly* seemed to be coming after, spending too much time looking back – whether to the Holocaust, the great modern masters or the elegiac glow of lost Jewish worlds. Where were the new voices and the new energy? When Alexander Baron looked around him in 1960, he saw "not only new attitudes but a new high level of talent". Could any contributor now, looking at Jewish culture in Britain, say the same thing?

Seventy years on from 1953, under Morry Schwartz, Jonathan Pearlman and Natasha Lehrer, there is a new *Jewish Quarterly*, in a new home, with a new vision and a formidable group of distinguished contributors and subjects, including Simon Schama, Deborah Lipstadt, Benjamin Balint on Paul Celan, Nir Baram, Deborah Levy, Richard J. Evans, Eva Hoffman, Tali Lavi on Cynthia Ozick, Adam Kirsch on new Jewish-American writing and George Prochnik on W.G. Sebald. There are big articles on geopolitics from the Israeli left to the new Middle East. We have come a long way from Worcester Crescent. *The Jewish Quarterly* is less British and less insular, more international and political than it's ever been. There is a new ambition, a new reach and new readers.

All this is admirable. But we should also remember our past. Once, many years ago, writers remembered how in Odessa they strolled along the beach with Bialik or remembered Manger, whom they first met in pre-war Warsaw. Gone but not forgotten. ≡

History

The Rambam and his brother

Harvey Belovski

It is the early 1170s, in Fustat (now Cairo), a major Nile port crowded with vessels and travellers from all over the world. Two brothers – Moshe and David Maimonides – have recently arrived from Morocco, joining the city's thriving Jewish community. Moshe, the elder by a decade, and now in his early thirties, is familiar to us now as the Rambam, arguably the most influential Jewish philosopher of all time; David is a jewel merchant about to embark on a lengthy business voyage across the globe. The pair are close, as evidenced by their correspondence – it is hard to imagine that Moshe is not at the docks to see his brother off.

Yet this is the last time the brothers will see other. Some months into his expedition, David's ship capsized in a storm, sinking – without survivors – in the Indian Ocean. Much of what we know about this tragic episode, the relationship between the Maimonides brothers, and the impact of David's death on Moshe comes from two extraordinary letters.

The first, from David to Moshe, was discovered in the 1950s among manuscript fragments brought from the treasury of the Ben Ezra Synagogue in Old Cairo (known as the Cairo Genizah) to Cambridge University in the 1890s by Solomon Schechter. Schechter was then a lecturer in Talmudics and a reader in

Rabbinics, but is better known today as the second president of New York's Jewish Theological Seminary from 1902 until his death in 1915.

Dated 22 Iyar (no year is mentioned, but the document is believed to have been written no later than 1171), the letter was penned at the Red Sea port of Aydhab, which David visited before the last phase of his voyage. Writing in Judeo-Arabic, David describes himself wandering the Aydhab market, distressed. He is concerned about how worried Moshe must be about him and yearns to see his brother again in happy circumstances. David is disappointed at the scarcity of wares to purchase at Aydhab, thus justifying his decision to embark on a long and inevitably dangerous sea voyage. He invokes God's assistance for the journey and feels confident that he will almost be in India by the time his letter reaches Moshe.

> *David's death clearly transformed Moshe's life*

The second letter was written by Moshe, some eight years after he received the news of David's death, to Yafet ben Elijah the Judge, a rabbi whom the Maimonides brothers had befriended on a stay in Acre. Maimonides described Yefet as wise, understanding and insightful, one of the leading lights of the Jewish community of Acre. Moshe writes of a series of misfortunes that had befallen him, including ill-health, financial loss and even an attempted murder. Despite these travails, Moshe reports that "the very worst thing that has happened to me from my birth until now is the death of the righteous man who drowned in the Indian Ocean while in possession of much money belonging to me and others; he left a young daughter and his widow in my care". Moshe continues:

> For around a year from when the terrible news reached me, I was confined to bed with a serious inflammation, fever and delirium, and I almost perished. From then until now ... I have been mourning unconsolably. How could I be consoled? He was my son, raised on my knees, my brother, my disciple. It was he who traded in the market, earning a living, while I dwelled securely. He was a Talmudic scholar and an expert grammarian. My only joy was to see him, yet the sun has set on all joy. He has gone to his final rest, leaving me distraught in a foreign country. Whenever I see his handwriting or one of his works, I become agitated and my sorrow is renewed.

David's death clearly transformed Moshe's life – his physical and emotional wellbeing, and his financial position. Indeed, the scholar Yitzchak Sheilat understood Moshe's letter to mean that he had been David's business partner and now all their wares were lost at sea.

There seems little doubt from Moshe's statement that David had enabled him to "dwell securely"; in other words, David's business had provided the financial support Moshe needed to devote himself to his Torah studies. It must be further presumed that, following David's death, Moshe had to earn a living for himself as well as his sister-in-law and niece.

It is often said that his brother's death forced the Rambam to give up the life of a Torah scholar and become a physician to support his family. Yet Moshe continued to produce works of great scholarship. What has been called his magnum opus – the *Mishneh Torah*, a vast compendium of Jewish law – was written across the time of his brother's death (between approximately 1168 and 1177). And Moshe penned his philosophical masterpiece – *The*

Guide for the Perplexed – years after David's death, between 1185 and 1191. Of Moshe's three greatest works, only his commentary to the Mishnah was produced before his brother's demise.

In fact, David's death may not have influenced Moshe's plan to practise medicine. We know he had already studied medicine and received clinical training in Fez (Morocco), prior to his arrival in Egypt. The dispute among historians is about whether he began practising as a doctor in Egypt prior to David's death or only in 1178. We know Moshe became an eminent doctor and, according to the Muslim historian and medic Ibn Abi Usaybi'a, served as the personal physician to the first sultan of Egypt and Syria, Saladin. In a celebrated letter to his translator Samuel ibn Tibbon written in 1199, Moshe notes that "my duties to the sultan are onerous. I am obliged to visit him every day, early in the morning and when he, one of his children or any of his harem are unwell."

The sudden change in Moshe's fortunes also raises questions about whether it shaped his position on individuals accepting financial support for studying Torah or for serving as a rabbi. Moshe's approach to this topic has been widely cited down the ages. It has been of particular interest to those arguing for (or against) a "professional" (that is, remunerated) rabbinate and whether communal funds should be used to support full-time Torah scholars.

In his commentary to the Mishnah, completed in 1168, before David's demise, the Rambam writes:

> Know that "do not make the Torah a spade with which to dig" means that one should not consider it an instrument from which to make a livelihood ... Anyone who benefits in this world from the honour of the Torah excises their soul from the next world. Yet people have closed their eyes to this clear statement ... and

they brought people to think in total error that one must help sages and students and those men who toil in the Torah, for whom Torah is their trade. All of this is an error that has no basis in the Torah.

Notwithstanding this hardline approach, it seems clear that Moshe himself accepted his brother's financial support for his Torah studies. It is therefore possible that Moshe's objection may apply only if the support is purely a gift, rather than a partnership in which the spiritual rewards of scholarship and the monetary rewards of business are shared. Alternatively, it may exclude support from an immediate family member. But neither of these hypotheses adequately reconciles Moshe's stated view with his own experience before David's death.

Moshe repeats his approach in *Mishneh Torah*: "One who decides to immerse in Torah study but not to work, and to support oneself from charity profanes God's name, deprecates the Torah, extinguishes the light of religion, brings evil on oneself and has eradicated one's life in the next world." Yet buried elsewhere in the *Mishneh Torah*, we find what appears to be a modification:

> Why were the Levites not allocated land in Eretz Yisrael or a share in its spoil along with their brothers? Because they were selected to serve the Lord and minister to him, to teach his upright ways and just laws to the public ... Not only the tribe of Levi, but any person at all who is so moved and intellectually driven to be distinct, to stand before the Lord, to serve Him, to worship Him, to know the Lord ... The Lord will give this person sufficient sustenance in this world, just as He gave to the Kohanim and the Levi'im.

Interestingly, the Rambam appears to hold that Torah teachers and leaders, as opposed to pure scholars, may receive support from others for their endeavours. Why is this exemption not mentioned in the Rambam's earlier commentary?

It is not possible to detect any direct influence of David's death on Moshe's approach. But at this later stage in his life, perhaps Moshe looked back at his privileged former life as a scholar "dwelling securely" with his brother's help and realised that, at least as far as teachers and potential spiritual leaders of the Jewish community are concerned, the support of others – cast here as "sufficient sustenance" from the Lord – was necessary, even desirable.

It is remarkable to think that the acclaim and influence which the Rambam attained for being both an eminent rabbinic leader and a famed doctor may never have materialised had his brother David not died in such tragic circumstances. It is also fascinating to consider the extent to which David's unexpected death and, with it, the Rambam's need to earn a living influenced his often-quoted approach to training and funding Jewish community leaders.

Community

The dybbuk in the room: Melbourne's Yiddish art scene

Tali Lavi

I would like to be clear about this. There are certain spaces in Melbourne or Naarm – its original name – where I have been privy to manifestations of the dybbuk. While varied in nature, my encounters with this mythic creature have all involved the collision of the Yiddish language with a radical form of artistic expression that can be traced back to Europe in the 1920s and 1930s but is also utterly modern. A renaissance in Yiddish culture is currently underway within this city, akin to the art of its antecedents: replete with contradictions, earthy and intellectual, erupting with chutzpah and a quivering energy.

The dybbuk's etymology lies in the Hebrew verb "to cleave". Spectral figures from the *Zohar* (the seminal text of Kabbalistic teaching), they are the lingering, discontented dead who possess the bodies of the living, later embedded in Hasidic tales that speak in hushed tones of the transmigration of souls. But it was not until S. An-ski's Yiddish play, inspired by his ethnographic expeditions through remote Yiddish hamlets in Ukraine in the early 1900s, that the dybbuk truly ignited the Jewish popular imagination. *The Dybbuk*'s central haunting occurs when Leah the bride is possessed by the wandering spirit of Channon, the young, indigent scholar who was in love with her. Once released onto the Warsaw stage, this dybbuk resisted containment, spreading across Europe (one of the troupes performing the play in 1921 had an estimated audience of 200,000). Later, Michał Waszyński's 1937 memorable adaptation translated it into celluloid.

This iteration of the dybbuk that An-ski awakened continues to linger, to await openings onto stages, oscillating between the sinister and the unearthly thrill of transformative possibilities. Its restless force speaks of the past's reluctance to loosen its hold and of a haunting by a world that is beyond our understanding.

The Shoah is a volcanic presence. Outside of Israel, this city has been home to the highest ratio of Holocaust survivors within its Jewish population. Approximately 32,500 Jews lived in Australia prior to the war (a third had migrated after 1933) and a further 23,000 arrived over the decade following its end. According to historian Suzanne Rutland, of these, around 60 per cent settled in Melbourne, Australia's second-most populous city. One might speculate that this mass experience of trauma, of loss and longing, formed an optimum habitat for a dybbuk breeding ground.

*

Here in Australia, in *Ek Velt* ("the end of the world"), Indigenous Australians are custodians of the land and one of the oldest living cultures in the world. The colonial violence underpinned by *terra nullius* – "the land of no one" – resulted in the dispossession and genocide – both physical and cultural – of First Nations peoples whose spirituality and rich storytelling traditions are replete with shapeshifting spirits.

For many Jewish migrants and exiles – including those descended from the first migrants, the First Fleet arrivals – Australia was imbued with this (fallacious) idea of unpopulated otherness.

Significantly, the country was distant from landscapes and people caustic with virulent antisemitism. The Yiddish phrase "*Ek Velt*" is telling: unlike the siren call of America's *Goldene Medina* ("The Golden Land"), choosing Australia, or being chosen by Australia, was tethered to the act of fleeing. In this antipodean fantasy, the place of refuge was devoid of lustre – the end of the world.

The Birrarung, "River of Mists", widely known as the Yarra River, traverses Melbourne. The Jewish story here has been contoured by the banks of this river: both the north and south sides have accommodated a shtetl. The trajectory of its movement across the water is mirrored in my mother's family's voyage. Their journey of flight originates in Soviet-controlled Prague and pauses in Vienna, where her sister is born. They embark upon the SS *Napoli* in Genoa. As the ship's ledger attests, most of the passengers are fellow Jews. Its emotional load is weighed down by tender devastations (and yet a photograph captures a birthday celebration). My mother is four years old when she and her family alight in Australia. Their destination is initially north of the river: Carlton, where Yiddish culture is thriving. It is 1950, and theatre legend Yankev Waislitz, "the walking windmill" – named for his vigorous arm movements, a commanding mix of migrant gesticulations and theatricality – is walking around Rathdowne Street, loudly reciting his lines in Yiddish. Waislitz has enough dybbuks to fill up the country. So do many inhabitants of Shtetl Carlton.

Searching for dybbuks, 2022

I join Melbourne author Arnold Zable for a ramble he has taken with numerous others before me, among them notables of the global Yiddish arts community. We meet at the gate of his childhood home, a workers' cottage in a row of now-gentrified houses. Behind the restored iron lacework are rooms in which Zable's mother sang Yiddish songs she had performed in her hometown of Bialystok while his father penned Yiddish poems. A house of longing and sighs, of suffering and dreams, of the suffocating presence of guilt.

We walk to a building that is strangely Moorish in influence. Built in 1933, the Kadimah Yiddish cultural institution was, says Zable, an "amazing citadel of culture". Yiddish letters are no longer emblazoned on it; since 1968 it has been a cultural centre for Melbourne's Aeolian community. The building faces a landscape of the dead, the Melbourne General Cemetery, its choice of location a prefiguring of the lost world of spirits the Kadimah once invoked in plays performed on a stage that has since been disassembled.

The Jewish Cultural Centre and National Library
Kadimah, Melbourne, c. 1941

With a voice inflected by Carlton, his cherished former neighbourhood, Zable conjures up a time when these streets thrummed with activity: a patchwork of working-class Australians and migrant Europeans. It is evening. The shtetl inhabitants spill from their homes after a gruelling workday to make their way to the Kadimah. It is akin to a sacred rite, though many are staunch secularists, and they are alive with anticipation for the theatre's epic transformative power. The ghosts issue forth from Zable, an indefatigable teller, writer of classics of Australian literature: *Scraps of Heaven*, *Cafe Scheherazade*, *The Fig Tree*, *The Watermill*. He is a bard of the dispossessed, a conduit for spectres that emerge from genocide and atrocity.

Zable's animus arises from his intense *menschlichkeit* (humanity) and the formidable stories for which his mind is a repository. In *Wanderers and Dreamers: Tales of the David Herman Theatre* he outlines Melbourne's place as the heart of Yiddish theatre in Australia – from the first Yiddish play performed in 1909, to the heyday of the David Herman Theatre at Kadimah in the 1930s to 1950s, through to the company's demise in 1992. It is a history bound to the experimental theatre of the famed Vilner Troupe and of the *Kleynkunst* (Yiddish cabaret). Exiled luminaries of these theatrical traditions, Yankev and Yocheved Waislitz and Rochl Holzer had taken refuge in this city prior to the Shoah, while Moishe Potashinski and Mila Waislitz arrived after its devastation.

If Zable and I were to continue walking, we would find ourselves outside the opulent Second Empire facade of the Princess Theatre, currently housing *Harry Potter and the Cursed Child*. In 1938, *The Dybbuk* played here to a capacity audience of 1500, Jews and non-Jews alike. Directed by Yankev Waislitz – who had performed in the play's 1920 debut in Warsaw, at the *shloshim* (the thirtieth day after a burial) of its creator, S. An-ski – it was a critical success.

Arguably, this was Melbourne's first mass witnessing of the dybbuk. European Jewry is on the cusp of conflagration. The dybbuk inhabiting Leah the bride onstage must be the lesser of the dybbuks in a room in which refugees are both actors and audience. Such is the horror and wonder of this scene. It threatens to still the heart.

*

In the late 1960s, recognising that most of the Jewish community had relocated south of the river, Kadimah moved to Elsternwick, a suburb whose streets are flanked by plane trees. It is there still. Around the corner is Sholem Aleichem College, a flourishing primary school founded in 1975 by Yiddishists and Bundists.

At Melbourne Jewish Book Week in 2022, in a session titled "Yiddish in Performance", Rebecca Margolis (a Canadian who is a professor at the Australian Centre for Jewish Civilisation and specialist in Yiddish culture at Monash University) referred to Sholem, pronouncing Melbourne to be the "only place in the world where Yiddish is being taught to children under the age of twelve in a secular context". She is impassioned when discussing the local Yiddish arts scene. While Yiddish has long been associated with wanderers and exiles, outsiders and rebels, longing and humour, Margolis says, the language has become a symbol around the world of queerness, of leftist politics, of an outsider identity. In this city, these associations are in dialogue with Yiddish's potency as a living language.

> *Unlike other global communities, the Melburnians breathing life into the language are not confined to the Haredi community*

Unlike other global communities, the Melburnians breathing life into the language are not confined to the Haredi community, who also largely reside in Elsternwick. A quickly growing constellation of mesmerising work has recently emerged from *Di Farborgene Khalyastre* ("The Gang of the Concealed"), a collective imagined by Dr Nathan Wolski, scholar of Kabbalah and Yiddish, and composed of musicians, poets and an artist. Their name bears tribute to the "avant-garde Yiddish poets of 1920s Warsaw". On their website, poet Aaron Zeitlin's radical provocation calls forth, "Yiddish art! Could be the messiah of arts." Zeitlin, who escaped Poland for New York in 1939 and whom Isaac Bashevis Singer described as "a veritable spiritual giant", was a prolific experimental writer in both Yiddish and Hebrew. There are echoes of antiquity and An-ski in the collective's intoxicating assemblage of art, song, mysticism and language. In *Di Farborgene Khalyastre*'s short film *Kaddish by the Ruins: A Liturgy*, Anita Lester's monochromatic artwork and the original score engage with Zeitlin's poetry of open wounds, which interrogates God and His world in the wake of the Shoah. It is a work of intense disquiet, a host for the dybbuks of Zeitlin and our murdered ancestors in their mother tongue.

Dybbuk sightings, Gilgul Theatre, The Exile Trilogy (1991–1993)

In 1991, the dybbuk makes the first of a series of appearances via the Gilgul Ensemble. The ensemble existed for six short years but still attained mythic status. It was dreamed up by a then 23-year-old Barrie Kosky and developed together with his collaborators, a diverse band of theatre provocateurs and artists. Gilgul's adaptation of *The Dybbuk* formed the first part of its *Exile Trilogy* and blasted open Melbourne's relationship to theatre. Critic Helen Thomson later claimed that *The Dybbuk* was so extraordinary, its radical vision so fully realised, that it shifted norms of theatrical critical conversation. The performances involved staggering physical feats; in one instance, Yoni Prior as Leah the bride appeared in a ceiling-high wedding dress on stilts.

Prior, now Honorary Senior Fellow in Theatre at the prestigious Victorian College of the Arts (VCA), acted in four of the five Gilgul productions. *Levad*, the last of the trilogy, was composed of her solo performance. It closely quoted Jacob Gordin's 1898 play *Mirele Efros*, originally known as *The Yiddish Queen Lear*. We meet in a café at the VCA. Its campus nestles into the city's arts precinct ("Cultural Capital" vies with "Garden State" in Melbourne's marketing campaigns). I ask Prior about Gilgul. My interest in it is voracious. I am haunted by regret – that I might have been, but was not, present at their shows.

The snippets of this work that exist on film, incorporated into Melissa Rymer's documentary *Kosky in Paradise* (1995), make me sicken with impossible nostalgia. Despite most of the ensemble members not being Jewish, they devised Jewish art that was fervid and audacious, highly European in its aesthetic, dense with visual artistry. Prior tells me that Gilgul "were explicitly drawing on the traditions of Yiddish Art theatre and *schund* – 'low', popularist theatre and cabaret". Yiddish songs disrupted the action. The company's layering of textual and historical references – the revolutionary Polish theatre of Tadeusz Kantor (particularly *The Death Class*), Yiddish theatrical lore, Jewish symbolism, stories and mysticism – and the robust collaborative process recalls a page of Talmud. One that has burst open and become animate.

The first Gilgul shows were created and performed at the far end of the spinal cord of Melbourne's second shtetl, south of the river. Carlisle Street in St Kilda is part-Jew, part-hipster, sometimes an amalgamation of both. In this it is reminiscent of Paris's Le Marais neighbourhood, although essentially limited to a single road; its tram lines are its most distinctive topographical feature. I regularly order lattes from Wall Two 80, a bustling café at its midpoint that used to be Waislitzer's kosher butcher. Original Hebrew "Kosher" signage is still displayed by its current occupants, who serve bacon and egg rolls in toasted challah buns. As a child I would enter with my mother and an older man would lean over the counter and ask the *meydele* if she would like a *shtikel* kabana, his voice resonant with the singsong qualities of a native Yiddish speaker. Three decades later, on this same street, another encounter would recall those childhood ones, this time in Glicks – a kosher bakery renowned for its bagels and its challah, closer to cake than bread. One of the last survivors from the Old Continent, whom I loved and who was beloved of many, was waiting to be served. He asked with the musicality of a Polish Yiddish speaker if he might buy me a *baygele* – never mind that I was in my early forties. Seeing him in that last decade of his life was to experience the pleasure of his impish presence and a concurrent wave of grief, as I recognised that this landscape would soon no longer be populated by these cadences, tinctured by their speakers' histories.

Kosky, who has claimed that Gilgul was his "fertile ground", is now a Europe-based opera director, mostly celebrated but also reviled: he cultivates the polarisation. Last June, before stepping down as decade-long artistic director of the Komische Oper Berlin, his final offering was the high-chutzpah, high-camp *Barrie Kosky's All Singing, All-Dancing Yiddish Revue*. Kosky was not born into a family of Yiddish speakers, but he emerged from a city saturated with their history.

Melbourne had allowed the Europe of An-ski and Kantor, of Kafka and Kosky, to take hold. But when *The Exile Trilogy* travelled to Sydney in 1993, its transgressive, esoteric nature didn't take root in the same way. The local Jewish community, mostly composed of Hungarians and their descendants, had no affinity with Yiddish. The dybbuk was diffused.

Dybbuk sightings, various venues, YID! (2017, 2018, 2019, ongoing)

A Yiddish big band. Flung into the air as a passing idea or perhaps a dare by Willy Zygier, it was taken up by Simon Starr. YID! is comprised of over twenty musicians including Zygier, Starr and his brother Adam. The band's name reappropriates an antisemitic slur, the exclamation mark bearing testimony to its joyous exuberance and volume. YID! is markedly Jewish even as many of its acclaimed musicians are not. As an aural experience, it is explosive; traditional modes of klezmer and cabaret fuse with spoken word, groove, jazz, free improvisation and electronica. At performances, carefully orchestrated anarchy is met by the breathlessness of its onlookers – a state not merely attributable to energetic dancing. The band has played to thousands at Adelaide's WOMADelaide festival and Toronto's Ashkenaz Festival.

> *The effect is thrilling and unsettling, a kind of corporeal and spiritual* tohu vavohu

In the audience at Memo Hall in St Kilda, 2018, are a smattering of Yiddish speakers born before their original world was obliterated. When band member Tomi Kalinski intones "*Es Brent*" ("It Burns"), accompanied by an eerie soundscape, some present are recollecting their embodied pasts. Written in 1938 by Polish poet Mordechai Gebirtig in response to a pogrom, "*Es Brent*" was rendered prophetic by the Shoah. Gebirtig was shot in the Kraków Ghetto. The song's direct admonition of bystanders "looking on" while the "shtetl burns" speaks of the past but contains the possible analogy to our own casual witnessing of catastrophe.

When Husky Gawenda sings a version of Paul Simon's migrant classic "*Der Boxer*", translated by his mother, Annie, his soulful tones declaw the dybbuk in the room. Perhaps it is averse to sweetness. Either way, it is always a burning presence at YID! concerts.

*

Gawenda, along with his sister Evie and their cousin Gideon Preiss (also a member of YID!), conceived of another Yiddish musical act, the Bashevis Singers. All former students at Sholem, they recently released their second album, *Soul Joy 1727*. They term it a "contemporary reimagining" of the oldest Yiddish songbook of the same name by Elkhonen Kirkhhan, published in 1727. Alongside songs of Shabbat and festivals, layered with influences as diverse as Leonard Cohen and Beastie Boys, surfaces the unmistakably Nirvana-esque track "*Malekhamoves*" ("Angel of Death").

Margolis conjectures that Melbourne offers a "fruitful performative space" because no individual or institution here owns or controls the Yiddish world. Perhaps the roots of this democracy lie in our physical remoteness from Europe and North America, which allows artists to develop unconstricted. Perhaps it is a manifestation of Australia's maverick spirit rubbing up against the Yiddish; its own singular version of chutzpah.

Dybbuk sighting, 23 March 2022, Fairfax Theatre

The *Yetser Ho're* (Evil Inclination) appears in a plush theatre and is speaking Yiddish. The effect is thrilling and unsettling, a kind of corporeal and spiritual *tohu vavohu*, the Biblical concept of chaos or the subversion of things. The source text is Isaac Bashevis Singer's short story "Yentl", which Kadimah Yiddish Theatre (KYT) has radically – but also faithfully – adapted into a work of the same name that feels like an execution of dark magic. Less Babs and Mandy, more Judith Butler colliding with the shtetl. My body reacts: hairs rise, gooseflesh forms. The uncanny is a fierce presence. In the days following, I cannot stop speaking of this extreme embodied reaction and find that others responded similarly.

KYT artistic director Evelyn Krape talks to me some months later in her home, which is in neither of Melbourne's shtetls. Her *Yetser Ho're* was a theatrical tour de force, a character assembled by the seasoned actor and the creative team: director Gary Abrahams; writers Abrahams, Galit Klas and Elise Hearst; Margolis as translator and designer Dann Barber. Although Krape's family's roots are bound up in the language – her grandmother spoke Yiddish, and she has memories of her parents bursting into Yiddish song – learning her Yiddish-dense lines for *Yentl* was gruelling. Krape speaks of the dybbuks in Singer's work. She acknowledges that Melbourne's intimate relationship with Yiddish and Yiddishkeit has been nourished by its shtetls.

KYT's *Yentl* garnered rave reviews. Rachel Chrapot, CEO of Kadimah, later tells me that the production "took us [Kadimah] out of the shtetl". If allowed (artistic rights are currently being sought), *Yentl* might tour and unleash its particular dybbuk into the rest of the world. While S. An-ski's play depicted the Yiddish culture and legends of Ukraine, it spoke to the audience's anxieties and their desires to enter a realm departed from realism. With its curtain inked like a Torah scroll and a backdrop honeycombed with glowing arched apertures, the *Yentl* set was one of openings – to the seductive world of the Kabbalah and the incendiary spirit, to a mythic and a historic world.

*

Yiddish was formed in a world now vanished, whose evocations seeped into the foundations of shtetls lapped by the waters of the Birrarung: first north, then south. Artists employing this language are conjuring this lacerated past and merging it with a modern sensibility. Into this charged terrain, the dybbuk steps. Within this city, we welcome it, opening ourselves, as if in collective memory, to its passage into narratives and pasts beyond our knowing, uncontainable by words. ▣

Reviews

Is Poland really forgetting its amnesia?
Jakub Nowakowski

Resurrecting the Jew: Nationalism,
Philosemitism, and Poland's Jewish Revival
Geneviève Zubrzycki
Princeton University Press

Tales from the Borderlands:
Making and Unmaking the Galician Past
Omer Bartov
Yale University Press

Let me start with a disclaimer. Geneviève Zubrzyckis's book is about me. Or, to be more precise, about people like me.

I come from a non-Jewish family that has lived for generations in Kazimierz, the Jewish quarter of Kraków. When I was growing up, we never talked about Jews at home. We felt neither sorrow nor satisfaction that the Jews were no longer there. The historic synagogues did not inspire awe in us. They were just a part of the landscape – which, in the late 1980s and early 1990s, was often pretty squalid.

And yet dinner was always cooked on a stove that my mother called the *szabaśnik* – the Shabbat oven. When I was naughty, she would yell "*Ty bachorze!*", unaware that she was using the Yiddish word *bachur*, meaning a boy. During important holidays we always ate fish cooked Jewish-style.

That's it. Unknowingly and unreflectively, we incorporated these random echoes of someone else's past into our present, into our daily lives.

My family was living in Kazimierz before the war, but most of our neighbours moved in after 1945. They appropriated the stagnant space, drowning out the resonating silence of the murdered Jews and filling this void with their stories, so there was no room for any other voices. We overwrote the history of the place, creating a kind of palimpsest of human fate.

Nonetheless, over time a change occurred. We began to see that the stories we told ourselves were incomplete. We began to ask questions. And, worse, we began to look for answers.

This history – beginning with the last decades of the Polish People's Republic and the first years of democratic Poland, when people were poor, fixated on their conviction of having experienced exceptional suffering, and uninterested in remembering their Jewish neighbours – is the necessary background for understanding the processes and transformations described by sociologist Geneviève Zubrzycki in *Resurrecting the Jew: Nationalism, Philosemitism, and Poland's Jewish Revival*.

Contemporary Polish–Jewish relations have long been Zubrzycki's field of interest. In 2006, she published *The Crosses of Auschwitz: Nationalism and Religion in Post-Communist Poland*, the genesis of which was the so-called war of the crosses, triggered by Catholic activists who placed crosses outside the grounds of the Auschwitz-Birkenau camp in 1998. Zubrzycki used this as the starting point for a comprehensive analysis of Polish–Jewish relations, the role of the Catholic Church in shaping them, and, above all, divergent visions of Polish identity in the first years of the democratic transition.

In *Resurrecting the Jew*, Zubrzycki returns to the subject, attempting to describe the landscape of contemporary Jewish Poland. The picture she draws is complex, perfectly capturing the ambiguity of phenomena that have shaped this reality over the past twenty years. She focuses on two distinct developments. The first is the growing interest of non-Jewish Poles in Jewish culture and their involvement in restoring the memory of Polish Jewry, alongside attempts to come to terms with the painful truth about the involvement of Polish Catholics in the persecution and deaths of their Jewish neighbours during World War II. Against this background she explores the second development: the rebirth of actual Jewish life in Poland, the attempts of this new Jewish community to define itself, and the challenges it faces.

Both developments have been noticed and, to some degree, scrutinised in national and international media. Reports either offer evidence of the age-old antisemitism of the Poles and their unwillingness to come to terms with past sins, or proof of the success of the transformation, the way Poland has welcomed the rebirth of Jewish life, demonstrating the tolerance and openness of Polish society and the scale of its integration of Western values. Polish Jews themselves, meanwhile, are still described mainly in relation to their traumatic past. Most headlines are along the lines of this one from a 2019 article in *Time*: "40 Miles from Auschwitz, Poland's Jewish Community Is Beginning to Thrive".

Zubrzycki, however, goes far deeper, asking fundamental questions about the significance of Poland's Jewish turn and of Polish philosemitism, without reducing either phenomenon to anti-antisemitism or a reaction to Poland's recent political shift to the right. Although her focus is Jewish Poland, Zubrzycki's observations and conclusions could be applied in completely different contexts. She seeks "to propose an approach to observing the making, unmaking, and redrawing of the symbolic boundaries of national identity".

The book is divided into two main parts. The first, entitled "The Great Mnemonic Awakening", analyses the processes of commemoration of Polish Jewry, driven today by non-Jewish Poles. Presenting examples of activities organised by artists, foundations, local government and museums, Zubrzycki paints a fascinating and intriguing picture. On the one hand, the book underlines the scale of the awakening, the polyphony of voices in which non-Jewish Poles speak about Jews. In many ways this is a positive interaction, fuelled by local activists who are, usually on their own initiative, working to preserve the last traces of Jewish heritage. Not only do they recognise that Jewish culture is part of their own identity, they also take pride in Poland's multicultural and multi-ethnic past.

Sometimes, however, the results of these activities are less positive. In most of the places where non-Jewish Poles organise festivals and commemorative programmes, erect monuments, clean cemeteries, open Jewish museums – there are no longer Jews. It is *we* – ethnic Poles – who spin our stories, sometimes real and sometimes invented, about Jews, and *we* – ethnic Poles – who listen. Some of these stories are meant to make us reflect on the complicated Polish-Jewish history, to encourage us to face our demons, to puncture the balloon of our "collective narcissism", which, as Agnieszka Golec de Zavala, a prominent social psychologist, describes, is the conviction that *our* nation is incomparably better than all others, and deserves recognition and glory. Such collective fantasies are not unusual; many nations suffer from similar obsessions. What distinguishes Poland's narcissism is its source: the conviction of our unparalleled courage and moral rectitude, overlaid with a narrative of exceptional suffering and martyrdom. This gives rise to a conflict between liberal forces driven by the so-called pedagogy of shame – an attempt to face the most difficult aspects of Polish–Jewish relations; and what one might call a pedagogy of pride – affirming the achievements of the Polish nation and glorifying a very narrow conception of patriotism.

The battleground on which this conflict is being played out is the memory of the Jews and Polish–Jewish relations. Paradoxically, the biggest challenge today is neither collective amnesia and a conspiracy of silence, as it was under Communism, nor the Polish authorities, against whom vociferous accusations of antisemitism are regularly made. Today the greatest threat is an increasingly common, artificial philosemitism – a selective and shallow admiration for a newly rediscovered Jewish culture, an incomplete version stripped of nuance that fits our vision of the past – hospitable and big-hearted Poland bringing help and salvation. In this narrative, Jews become a convenient tool with which we Poles can manifest our generosity, courage and sacrifice. We *need* Jews because they give us heroes to feed our collective narcissism. We put these heroes – our Ulmas, Sendlers and Karskis – on the shoulders of the Jews and make them carry these figures out into the world – not to tell the story of Jewish suffering, but as proof of our Polish bravery and heroism.

Zubrzycki is correct when she writes that "Jewish absence feeds the nightmares of the Right and their negative stereotypes of Jews as well as the dreams of the Left. The absent Jewish body is an empty container, filled with Polish aversions, fears, desires, and aspirations." She describes this as a clash between secular and Catholic Poland, especially in the context of the entanglement of the Polish Church with the current right-wing government and the brutal, advancing encroachment of the Church into the private lives of Poles. Nonetheless, the division is not so simple: one distinct group of people interested in Jewish culture, involved in its revival and treating it with utmost respect, in the spirit of the thought of Pope John Paul II, is churchgoing Catholics. Although sometimes their activities can be difficult to comprehend, they are actively involved not only in keeping Christian–Jewish dialogue open, but also in stigmatising antisemitism among the clergy. Zubrzycki rightly emphasises the scale of the involvement of non-Jews, which far exceeds anything happening in other European countries or the United States. This is exemplified by the tens of thousands of ordinary Varsovians who commemorate the anniversary of the Warsaw Ghetto Uprising each year, or the thousands who participate in the annual Kraków Jewish Culture Festival. And this mass interest in the culture and heritage of Polish Jews is far from just a metropolitan phenomenon. There are activists in small towns, cleaning up Jewish cemeteries or erecting monuments dedicated to the memory of their former Jewish neighbours. We are witness today to an unstoppable process of acknowledging the simple fact that we live in post-Jewish spaces.

An excellent example of this can be seen in the recently opened museum in Biecz, a charming little town some 100 kilometres east of Kraków. The museum is located on the market square opposite the town hall, in the basement of a former synagogue. Before the Holocaust, Jews made up 15 per cent of the population. The synagogue's central location speaks volumes about the pre-war community's visibility and importance. The exhibition opens with an aerial photograph of the square, taken just before the outbreak of World War II. Each building is described with the names of its former inhabitants, the vast majority of them Jewish. Today there are no Jews in Biecz, and the houses where they once lived belong to Poles. The creators of the exhibition, local historians and artists, are no longer afraid of confronting the past.

Zubrzycki rightly notes that the "resurrection of Jewish culture is primarily made by Poles, for Poles, and in the name of Polish culture". However, the second part of the book focuses on Polish Jews – the ones who are alive. Over the last twenty years, Jewish life has gradually returned to Poland. Zubrzycki asks fundamental questions about the identity of contemporary Polish Jews, exploring some of the problems and challenges they face as a community and tracing lines of division and internal conflicts, such as over who represents them. The rebirth of Jewish life in Poland is not only about returning to pre-war roots, as Katka Reszke, quoted in the book, puts it so well: "Jewish culture in contemporary Poland is not a returning phenomenon. It is a new construct, which very much relies on its past renderings and aspires to be rooted, to be a continuation."

Polish-Jewish roots were scorched during the Holocaust. The destruction was completed in the post-war years, with violent antisemitic pogroms and the purge of the late 1960s that resulted in the final breaking of the transmission belt by which identity is passed on from generation to generation. A constellation of daily customs, small gestures and words that set the Jews apart and made their lives unique was gone. The past had been erased. As a result, the Polish-Jewish narrative can appear diametrically different to those of Jews from Israel, the United States or the former Soviet Union. Zubrzycki notes that when she accompanies a group of

Polish Jews on their Birthright trip to Israel, they find themselves constantly having to explain their choice to remain living in the "land of ashes", in the "shadow of Auschwitz".

The question of the future for Polish Jews (or Jews in Poland) is again being reshaped in the context of the war in Ukraine and the influx of millions of refugees, including Ukrainian Jews. How will this affect the changes that have been taking place in Polish-Jewish communities? And how will the focus shift in terms of commemorating the Holocaust, considering the often very different experiences of Jews from the former USSR?

Perhaps this could be a future subject of study for Zubrzycki. Before that, however, it is worth getting acquainted with this insightful analysis. Zubrzycki can at times be brutally frank, but this is precisely why the picture she paints is so sharp and thought-provoking, encouraging the reader to re-evaluate their understanding of contemporary Polish–Jewish relations and Jewish life in Poland.

*

Yehuda Loew ben Bezalel, the famous Maharal of Prague and, according to legend, the creator of the Golem, wondered why the first letter of the first word of the Torah is Bet, ב. Why did the Creator start with the second letter of the alphabet and the corresponding number two? Bezalel found the answer in the duality of the letter: everything must be understood in two ways – what is visible, along with its hidden, secret, indeterminate meaning.

It so happens that the letter B is also the first letter of Buczacz, a town now in western Ukraine, to which historian Omer Bartov has devoted considerable attention over the years. *Tales from the Borderlands* is not simply another book about Buczacz, but a starting point for an intimate journey through the visible and the hidden, what is tangible and what is no longer there – in particular, what of the Jewish history of the former borderlands of the *Rzeczpospolita* (the Kingdom of Poland) is remembered or forgotten. Over more than 300 pages, Bartov not only documents the past, but tries to unveil the secret, hidden meaning of the stories associated with Buczacz and, more broadly, former Eastern Galicia. "It is the history of the men and women who populated the universe of the borderlands, their fates and hopes, dreams and disillusionment," writes Bartov. "But perhaps even more importantly, it is also a history of the stories they told themselves and others about who they were, where they came from, and where they were heading."

Straddling the margins of the empires that ruled them, and inhabited by diverse populations, these borderlands were a melting pot where Catholics, Jews and Ruthenians/Ukrainians communed with each other over centuries. This multitude of experiences and cacophony of voices translated into a rich cultural heritage, and an influence on the outside world despite the peripheral location. But diversity also meant tension, conflict and violence. Although Jews were the main victims of regularly recurring acts of violence – wars, pogroms or persecutions – the borderlands were also an area of constant friction between Poles, Ukrainians, Russians and Turks. In this regard, Bartov's book is terrifyingly relevant today.

Bartov does more than merely recall descriptions of violent events; he seeks to outline their genesis and explore their effect on contemporary relations between the descendants of the people who once inhabited the area. The memory of this complex community involves layers of emotions, stories and legends that are constantly being written over – not only by those who were born there, but also by those born elsewhere, much later, like Bartov himself, who was born in Israel in 1954.

The relationship we have to the places we come from matters. It is in these places that we define ourselves, confirm existing ties and sometimes build new ones. This act of symbolically embracing, or taking back possession of, one's heritage can be uplifting, prompting reflection on the often improbable complexities of human destiny. But it can, and often does, lead to conflict and rivalry. Arriving at these remembered places, we discover that they echo with the voices of others, strangers who have built their homes on the ruins of our world. We look at one another with suspicion, distrust and hostility, through the prism of past wrongs, real or imagined.

This is evident in the Ukrainian–Jewish relationship, marked by centuries of prejudice and stereotypes. "These polar perspectives have seeped through the generations well into the modern age," Bartov writes, "so while the stereotype of Ukrainian as barbaric murderers became part of the Jewish collective memory and representation, anti-Jewish stereotypes merging religious prejudice and popular superstitions with economic resentment and new ideologies became part and parcel of the … Ukrainian national literature." Understanding the origins of these beliefs is of particular importance today, when the entire free world supports the Ukrainian struggle against the Russian invasion. However, unequivocal support for the Ukrainian people does not always come easily and may be accompanied by discomfort caused by a historical dislike of Ukrainians passed down from generation to generation.

The history of the Jews, their pre-war presence and the Holocaust itself was erased from the curriculum in all the countries of communist Eastern Europe. Monuments were erected commemorating the *innocent victims*, never mentioning that they were Jewish. Synagogues, *mikvehs* and cemeteries became inconvenient witnesses to a past that people did not want to remember.

The situation only began to slowly change in the 1990s after the collapse of the Soviet Union. In Ukraine, however, this process of restoring memory was more complicated than, for example, in neighbouring Poland, because the country, formally established in 1991, desperately tried to prove the *right of ownership*, the fact of the existence of Ukrainian national heritage. This was done in the only possible way – by erasing traces of the presence of other people who once inhabited these lands, primarily Poles and Jews. "I first saw and photographed the tree [a legendary tree remembering Polish kings] on a gloomy, overcast day in October 2008, just after visiting the nearby, newly erected monument to Stephan Bandera," Bartov writes.

> Leader of the Organization of Ukrainian Nationalists, Bandera was intimately linked to the explosion of violence that sealed the fate of Buczacz as a community of several ethnicities and faiths; he represents a generation in which brother turned against brother and torrents of blood were shed in the name of purity, liberty, and justice. The tree had seen it all; but the people in the banged-up cars driving on the road next to it, or those in their crumbling apartments across the untended lawn ... remembered none of it.

Fortunately, over the past few years, this mass amnesia has begun to fade, though probably not yet everywhere. A new generation has emerged in Ukraine, proud of its multicultural past and ready to talk fearlessly about the complicated history of its homeland. Although this generation and these people do not appear in *Tales from the Borderlands*, Bartov nevertheless sheds light on complicated Ukrainian–Jewish relations, outlining the sources of hatred and stereotypes. It offers hope, for Ukrainians as well as Jews and Poles, that perhaps we can break out of our predetermined roles. Therein lies its extraordinary importance, especially now, as war continues in Ukraine.

Fortunately, Bartov doesn't define the historic borderlands only through suffering and violence. He also writes about the cultural richness and diversity of the region, as well as the courage of some of the people who lived there, dreaming of changing the world. *Tales from the Borderlands* is peopled by Jews, Ukrainians and Catholic Poles, witnesses to and participants in the events unfolding around them. One of the main narrators is Buczacz-born Shmuel Yosef Agnon, born Shmuel Yosef Czaczkes, arguably the twentieth century's most important writer in Yiddish and Hebrew. Hailing from a traditional family, Agnon soaked up the stories and legends of the borderlands. He settled permanently in Palestine in the 1920s, but his work was always marked by a longing for the "old land", as well as a crisis of identity and his own religiosity in the context of Zionism, characteristic of many immigrants of that generation.

For both Agnon and Bartov, Buczacz and the borderlands are marked by indelible scars of sorrow and suffering, despite their beauty and rich history. This duality (as we know from the letter B in the city's name) is always evident in Agnon's work: "For those familiar with Agnon's voluminous writings on his hometown, this idyllic perception was always mixed with another, far more critical view," Bartov observes. "In much of his fiction, Agnon does not call the town by its real name but rather refers to it as Shiush, a name derived from the Hebrew word for 'disruption, going wrong, going astray, or deviating'." Bartov also never allows the reader to forget that the world he is describing is doomed. Before the Holocaust, Buczacz and the surrounding areas were home to a vibrant and diverse Jewish population living in a complicated relationship with its non-Jewish neighbours. Echoes of their intertwined destinies are evident in Bartov's accounts of other figures, both Jews and non-Jews. Their life choices, dilemmas and struggles are a testament to the diversity of experiences, opportunities and ideas, as well as the ever-changing conditions in which they lived. Indeed, this was one of the sources of the richness of this world: the feverish ferment, the constant movement, the searching for a better way, the hopes and illusions that repeatedly ignited successive generations of idealists and rebels with the same fervour.

Bartov takes the reader the back to the turn of the twentieth century, when Zionism and assimilation were beginning to gain popularity among the Jewish masses. Turbulent conflicts erupted within the Jewish community, and the nationalist ideas prevalent throughout Europe further intensified tensions among ethnic and national groups living in the Austro-Hungarian empire. For Jews, this meant a tragic paradox. The empire created space for assimilation, which was supposed to allow Jews to become part of modern society. The reaction to growing assimilation, however, was not widespread acceptance, but a virulent and toxic antisemitism that defined Jews not by religion but by race. The greater the successes of assimilated Jews in intellectual or economic fields, the greater the fear, anger and hatred felt by the growing number of antisemites and nationalists, hijacked by the ideology of homogeneous nations and homelands. "The path to catastrophe was paved with good intentions, as well as rage and resentment: lifting the downtrodden entailed removing the alien; social justice required eliminating parasites; and love of country was demonstrated through sacrifice and blood."

Bartov describes the events of World War II and the Holocaust from the perspective of those who managed to escape it, including his own family. The starting point for the final, deeply moving chapter is the recording of a conversation in 1995 with his mother:

> At the time members of my generation in Israel, then in their forties, began realizing that they knew practically nothing about the world their parents had come from; they never asked, and their parents did not tell. And so, late one Friday morning, I came into my mother's kitchen, put my six-month-old-daughter in her chair by the table, told my seven-year-old son to play in the living room, pressed the recording button on the tape recorder, and asked my mother to tell me about her childhood.

The taped conversation became not only a source of information about the family and the difficult conditions they faced after arriving in Palestine, but also a testament to the unremitting longing and grief for the world they left behind. The Bartov family left Buczacz only a few years before the outbreak of war. Various cousins, uncles and more distant relatives stayed behind; almost none survived the Holocaust. What remains of them are yellowed letters, telegrams and photographs, and memories that will eventually vanish along with the last of those who recall them. Bartov and his mother's conversation, the range and detail of the descriptions, and perhaps the entire book are an attempt to capture these memories, to put them on paper and, fleetingly, to resurrect the dead.

But recounting the past has another meaning, especially in the context of the history of Eastern European Jews. Anthropologist

Paul Connerton, who died in 2019, noted that "through claiming who we are in relation to our past, we legitimize a particular social order and claim a particular understanding of the reality and our rights, relations and responsibilities". *Tales from the Borderlands* is an affirmation of the right to tell its stories and the right to be present in its history. The past – retold, repeatedly – is in constant flux, reflecting our desires, longings and fears. It is also subject to constant competition. Like the letter Bet, it has a secret, double, indeterminate meaning. Bartov and his latest book are excellent guides through its meanderings.

The myth of the Jewish literary mafia
Devorah Baum

The Literary Mafia: Jews, Publishing,
and Postwar American Literature
Josh Lambert
Yale University Press

"Perhaps some smart-ass fellow should write a book called *The Literary Mafia*," reads the epigraph of Josh Lambert's *The Literary Mafia: Jews, Publishing, and Postwar American Literature*. It's a smart-ass epigraph, alright – taken from a letter written by Robert DeMaria Sr to Ann Birstein on 30 November 1976, around the time when all the talk was of a *Jewish* literary mafia. Back then, you were just as likely to hear conspiracy theorists mouthing off about Jews running the book industry as you are today about Jews running Hollywood. Which figures, I suppose: Jews became the people of the blockbuster as well as of the world's number-one bestseller only fairly recently. But while Jews showed up early for the American film business, they didn't really begin making waves in the American book business until just after the World War II. That's what *The Literary Mafia* is about. By looking at the role Jews have played in shaping American letters, Lambert's book is also a record of the relatively short span of history that saw a minority group of ethnic outsiders enter the mainstream and become insiders in an exemplary but never yet replicated case of what he terms cultural enfranchisement.

Come to think of it, "Cultural Enfranchisement: A Case Study" could have been the title for Lambert's book. It would have been the politer choice, certainly, compared with the provocation of the actual title, which slightly unnerved me, as an angst-ridden European rather than a balls-to-the-wall American Jew, even before I read the first page and learned that the alleged existence of a Jewish literary mafia was a constant complaint of various American authors whom I had never suspected of saying such things before. Yet writers no less acclaimed than Jack Kerouac, Mario Puzo, Katherine Anne Porter and Truman Capote did, it turns out, go on and on about the Jewish racketeers they believed to be gatekeeping publishing in such a way as to advance only their own narrowly ethnic interests. *It's the Jews who control all the quarterlies and magazines... It's the Jews who make you or break you... American publishing is a Jewish conspiracy!* Sheesh. This kind of talk could get a girl down if it weren't for the fact that we don't usually hear such things said aloud by bookish people anymore. But then along comes a title like this one, and with it the obvious question: why bring the essentially antisemitic canard of a Jewish literary mafia back into public consciousness – especially now, when antisemitism seems to be making a ferocious comeback too?

Lambert's rationale for taking the allegation of the Jewish literary mafia seriously, even as he rejects the conspiratorial and antisemitic mindset that coined the term, is because the story he tells is ultimately that of how the "literary access" attained by post-war American Jews undermines the conceit that publishing is some sort of meritocracy. Recognising this, according to Lambert, is particularly important for an industry that often claims to want inclusivity for diverse minorities but does very little that isn't tokenistic to back it up. It would be wrong, however, to mistake his project here. He is not arguing that publishing *should* be meritocratic. What he is saying is that it *cannot* be, and that the illusion that it could be is precisely what holds the industry back. Literature, far from being an exact science, alludes to a realm of life and experience that is by nature subjective. And the subjective is, whether we like it or not, made up of all that we have inherited and made of our histories, our communities and our positions in the world. If aesthetic values and judgements are always going to be inflected with the cultural sensibilities of the person making them, there surely is, or at least can be, *some* accounting for taste.

While those who claimed there was a Jewish literary mafia were not necessarily wrong, then, to note that Jews could be found rubbing shoulders across sectors of American publishing, they *were* wrong to treat something normal as if it was nefarious. Observing that Jews often have a Jewish sensibility isn't exactly a profound insight. What other sensibility *should* they have? If only their accusers had been willing, writes Lambert, to acknowledge that every editor, critic and reader "regularly draws on their own background and experiences ... it would be harder for them to criticize such people, either individually or collectively, for at times favoring books by people who are like them or for hiring people who remind them of themselves". Lambert takes his own work as illustrative of this wider point. In his long acknowledgements, he identifies a slew of fortunate personal connections that enabled him to research, write and publish a Jewish-themed book with a major university press (a remark I can only make blushingly as someone who has also published a Jewish-themed book with the same university press). As such, what he acknowledges is a remarkable and admirable intervention.

Still, I have a small niggle. Admitting to owing one's breaks to a predominantly ethnic network that, however "fuelled by goodwill and generosity", might nonetheless be regarded as complicit in perpetuating inequality somewhat undermines the very safety and assurance it seems to announce. Since, in other words, it's generally only those who can sense how provisional their privileges are who are bothered to check them, you could say that here is a book with a very Jewish acknowledgements section in more ways than one.

Notwithstanding his lengthy acknowledgements, however, Lambert remains crystal clear on this point: an "ethnic niche" that has established networks within a particular industry, though it might mean opportunities for some, does not amount to a conspiracy. And that is revealed in part by the way ethnic niches don't always operate in the manner one might expect. A lot of Jews, for example, will have an idea of someone they consider the *wrong type* of Jew (as in, the type of Jew they fear reflects badly on them), meaning that some Jews wanting to gain a foothold in literary culture may well find it is the *Jewish* gatekeepers who are inclined to shut the door in their face. Lambert indeed includes examples of Jews, such as disgruntled writers Meyer Levin and Richard Kostelanetz, who themselves lamented the existence of this same imagined Jewish literary mafia. He also reflects on aspects of Jewish literary culture that manifest if not outright antipathy towards Jewish books and writers, then certainly ambivalence. Interwar editors at Alfred A. Knopf, for instance, the Jewish-owned publishing house founded in New York in 1915, though happy enough to publish works about European Jews, studiously avoided publishing books about the American Jewish experience – not wanting to "draw too much attention", as one editor put it. These were American Jews who fretted (as I still do, a bit) about books bearing titles like this one. Lambert then reveals even more disturbing evidence of Knopf's ambivalence towards Jewishness, hinging not so much on the books that were excluded from their lists, but the books that weren't. It seems to have been the culture at Knopf not to bat an eyelid when it came to publishing books containing antisemitic passages, including works by such renowned writers as Willa Cather, T.S. Eliot (whose notorious "Burbank with a Baedeker: Bleistein with a Cigar", with its infamous line "The rats are underneath the piles./ The jew is underneath the lot", Knopf published not once but twice), Raymond Chandler and H.L. Mencken – all of whom, when accused of antisemitism, had the perfect alibi: *Some of my best publishers are Jewish.*

The real question is why would anyone assume otherwise? Ethnic niches, much like ethnicities, are hardly monoliths, and they are no less likely to suffer the narcissism of small differences, or the conflicts that can fissure shared identities. Besides, any family business, or any Jewish family business at any rate, will, sure as night follows day, arrive at its Oedipal moment. At Knopf that moment came in 1959, when Alfred Knopf Jr, frustrated by his parents' reluctance to publish unapologetically Jewish titles, left the company to establish his own publishing house, Atheneum – a successful move that gave expression to the post-war American Jew as a character possessing a "more comfortable, jokey, and embracing attitude towards Jewishness". It's an attitude I tend to associate with such giants of post-war American Jewish literature as Bernard Malamud, Saul Bellow, Grace Paley, Philip Roth and Cynthia Ozick, and I can also detect it in Lambert's own embrace of the freedom, daring and optimism that characterised that brief golden age of American Jewish writing. For like, say, Roth, Lambert clearly is not afraid to portray real Jews, warts and all (his book includes portraits of such flawed but fascinating characters as Gordon Lish and Lionel Trilling). And like Roth too, he writes with the confidence that books written *by* Jews *about* Jews will be read and understood in the spirit the writer intended them. One might call this the American Jewish literary dream – a dream I am forever grateful for. It even brings to mind Roth's quip vis-à-vis his nervier or angrier Jewish critics, that he had yet to receive a letter of thanks from any antisemitic organisation.

What *The Literary Mafia* is really about, in the end, is progress, and how the history of the Jewish ethnic niche within publishing might have wider lessons for an industry in which progress seems to have stalled. But it is just as much a story of Jewish progressivism, including some trenchant observations regarding where that, too, has stalled. This is terrain that Lambert treads carefully, by analysing, for instance, the *romans à clef* of Jewish women – Rona Jaffe, T. Gertler and Ann Birstein – covertly reporting on Jewish #shittymediamen long before that hashtag came into existence in 2017, or by investigating why so many American Jewish writers of the post-war years won the National Book Award. Was that too the work of the literary mafia, he wonders. Not if you consider that it was by and large non-Jewish and non–New Yorker juries that awarded the prize to Jewish authors and Jewish books. Although there was one case where the Jewishness of the judging panel does seem to have swung it, if in an unexpected direction. This was in 1953, when three out of five judges were Jews: Saul Bellow, Irving Howe and Alfred Kazin. On their shortlist they had works by Ernest Hemingway and William Carlos Williams, along with Peter Martin's *The Landsmen*, a novel of nineteenth-century Jewish life in Eastern Europe. Yet the three men fought to award the prize to Ralph Ellison's *Invisible Man* – an award critical not only for Ellison, but also for the whole history of African American literature. Ellison, his biographer remarked, "was lucky in having three young, progressive Jewish writers as a majority on the panel", two of whom were his friends. But were the Jewish judges really involved in a literary version of that antisemitic trope, the great replacement conspiracy? It would be a hard case to argue, I reckon, given that they awarded the prize to what is, unequivocally, a masterpiece. But since it is true that the jury awarded the prize to someone "grappling with his relationship to minority experience and to a history of persecution and literary marginalization" – if it was the Jewish judges in particular who recognised the greatness of Ellison's work – then it is probably not such wild speculation to wonder if some shared ethnic sensibility may have had something to do with it.

I love that anecdote. It reminds me that books, or good books, are never really written for insiders. If Jews, traditionally, are the people of the book, it's because the book is the home of the literal or metaphorical exile – the type of person whose literary sensibility is always to some extent *outsider*, whether we're talking about Ellison, Malamud or Ozick, Kerouac, Puzo or Capote, Chandler, Cather or T.S. Eliot. And so, while I deeply appreciated Lambert's rich and subtle portrait of what remains distinctive about American Jewish literary culture, I also found myself reflecting that publishing, and even literature itself, in the context of a dominant *non*-literary culture, might likewise be regarded as its own sort of ethnic niche. ▤

www.ingramcontent.com/pod-product-compliance
Lightning Source LLC
Chambersburg PA
CBHW022148160426
43197CB00009B/1476